THE SHADOW PATH

THE SHADOW PATH

*A Journey to Uncovering Your Depths
and Illuminating Your Full Potential*

CHELSEY
PIPPIN MIZZI

BLUEBIRD

First published 2025 by Bluebird
an imprint of Pan Macmillan
The Smithson, 6 Briset Street, London EC1M 5NR
EU representative: Macmillan Publishers Ireland Ltd, 1st Floor,
The Liffey Trust Centre, 117–126 Sheriff Street Upper,
Dublin 1, D01 YC43
Associated companies throughout the world
www.panmacmillan.com

ISBN 978-1-0350-5568-5

1 3 5 7 9 8 6 4 2

A CIP catalogue record for this book is available from the British Library.

Illustrations by Sinead Hayward

Typeset in Warnock Pro by Palimpsest Book Production Limited, Falkirk, Stirlingshire
Printed and bound by CPI Group (UK) Ltd, Croydon, CR0 4YY

Visit **www.panmacmillan.com/bluebird** to read more about all our books
and to buy them. You will also find features, author interviews and
news of any author events, and you can sign up for e-newsletters
so that you're always first to hear about our new releases.

For all the parts of myself I'm out with
lanterns looking for.

'Perhaps all the dragons in our lives are princesses who are only waiting to see us act, just once, with beauty and courage. Perhaps everything that frightens us is, in its deepest essence, something helpless that wants our love.'

– Rainer Maria Rilke, *Letters to a Young Poet*

'I am out with lanterns looking for myself.'
– Emily Dickinson, in a letter to Elizabeth Holland

'How can I be substantial if I do not cast a shadow? I must have a dark side also if I am to be whole.'
– C.G. Jung, *Modern Man in Search of a Soul*

CONTENTS

INTRODUCTION:
THE OTHER HALF OF YOU

No matter what day or time you read this, there will be a full moon in the sky.

This is true because even when the moon is on the other side of the world, even when it appears in slivers and bites, the moon is always a complete object.

You may only see what the light reveals, or what your personal vantage point allows. But it's always there, the whole of it. New, full and in between, the moon does its work: it drags the tide and stabilizes the tilt of the earth's axis.

The funny thing is that even when we call it full, we only see the half of it. The dark side of the moon is always hiding on the other side of its bright, full face.

The funnier thing is that your soul works the same way. You were born whole. You exist in full. You experience the entire range of what it is to be human. You are always all of you, even when you're only showing up to the world – to yourself – in slivers and bites.

Not dissimilar to the moon, you only know the half of you.

That other half is called your Shadow, and it contains all of the mystery, power, magic and potential that make you extraordinary.

It's waiting to meet you, and this book will light your way as you set off on your path to discover yourself at your fullest.

Are you ready to take off into the dark and find yourself along the Shadow Path?

WHAT IS SHADOW?

Shadow is everything about us that is hidden in the unconscious – the depths of your psyche that you don't have automatic access to. It consists of all the buried parts of yourself: fears and repressed desires, but also your latent talents, gifts and a deep capacity for joy. This book is a guide to exploring and engaging with your Shadow, and recovering the buried things hidden within it.

In Psychology

The modern concept of Shadow is rooted in twentieth-century analytical psychology – beginning with the work of Sigmund Freud, who is widely considered to be the father of modern psychology, and the inventor of talk therapy as we know it. Freud's major theory of the mind separates the human psyche into three elements you may have heard of: the ego, or the conscious human mind; the id, which represents the unconscious parts of the mind; and the superego, which flits between the conscious and unconscious parts of the psyche. In his writings about what lies in those unconscious parts, Freud introduced the word 'shadow' as a metaphor for some dark psychological experiences.

But it was really Freud's student, Carl Jung, who put Shadow on the psychological map.

Jung popularized the phrase 'shadow self' and dedicated

a significant amount of his research and practice to developing modes of bringing the Shadow to light so that his patients could better heal.

Freud's writing on the subject casts shadow as a shorthand for negative elements and experiences – his take on shadow concerns the 'unlikeable' parts of us that we repress and hide away in our unconscious, and the dark fears we project onto others. Mainstream culture has absorbed this negativity around Shadow . . . defining the hidden parts of ourselves as vice, weakness, darkness – things that need to be excised.

But the hidden parts of us are so much more than shameful secrets.

In his work, Jung applied more compassion and possibility to the role of Shadow in our lives, positing that just because we've been told something about us is unsavoury, that doesn't mean it has to be rejected, or that it holds no value or beauty.

Today, there is no one way to speak about or offer Shadow Work as a healing modality. Psychologists' and Shadow Work practitioners' approach to Shadow varies, depending on how they were trained and what their clients want to achieve. For example, as a tarot reader and Shadow Work practitioner, the work I do will be markedly different from a clinical psychologist's approach. When looking for a therapist or practitioner to work with, it's important to ask them if, and how, they conduct Shadow Work with their clients, and consider whether or not their approach feels right for you before committing to work with them long term.

In Spirituality

Shadow isn't a concept exclusive to modern psychology – it's been a core tenet of many spiritual practices throughout history. The roots of the word 'occult' translate approximately to 'what is hidden in shadow' and date back to the Middle Ages. This tells us that mystics and magicians understood – and sought out – the power of what lies beneath the surface of our understanding for centuries before Freud and Jung came along.

Occultic and spiritual traditions, like Tarot, folk magic, meditation and manifestation practices have long acknowledged that the more willing we are to look into our depths and uncover what is hidden beneath our surface, to see the light and the darkness within ourselves, then the more peace we'll make with ourselves and our world, and the more power we'll have to make the changes we really want to see in our lives and our relationships.

Regardless of whether you come to Shadow from a more psychological or spiritual approach, you should know that your Shadow can be both a psychic location and an entity. It's somewhere you put things, but it's also something you communicate with. It plays different roles, and as you wander deeper down the Shadow Path, its role will evolve and flex. Rather than fight its shifting nature, I invite you to appreciate and celebrate it, to wonder at how incredible, how generous it is that your Shadow can morph into whatever you need it to be.

In this book, I've endeavoured to offer multiple perspectives about Shadow, and provided exercises rooted in an array of approaches, from Jungian and Freudian psychology to witchcraft to meditation and mindfulness to creativity coaching techniques, so that you can experiment with what feels right and true for you.

MY SHADOW JOURNEY

As a writer and artist, I've always been compelled by what lies underneath the surface that people present to others. When I studied theatre as an undergraduate, my favourite part of putting together a production was the 'table work' stage. Here, the actors and director take time before getting a play on its feet to interrogate the text, working to uncover what's going on beneath the surface – the subtext of each line, the hidden motivations of each character, the pulsing 'why' that animates the action.

I went on to study culture and philosophy as a master's student, and eventually wrote a dissertation about how theatrical performance allows us to signify emotional and spiritual exchanges that otherwise remain obscured in the daily humdrum of human experience. Jung and Freud's theories of the unconscious played a significant role in my argument.

And yet, despite my creative and academic fascination with how we bring what is unsaid and unknown to the surface, I remained terrified and avoidant of what lay in my own, seemingly impenetrable, depths.

It was only when I learned to read tarot cards at the end of my twenties that I discovered a language and method for speaking to my own depths. That's when my personal Shadow journey began.

Some tarot readers take special notice of cards that come out of the deck upside down. In this tradition, the 'reversed' interpretation of the image represents the 'shadow' side of the card; all of the dark, unsavoury pathways the card brings up. While this can be an interesting and stimulating way to read the cards, my understanding and approach to both the Tarot and Shadow Work was overhauled when a mentor told me: 'you don't need to read reversals when you realize everything a card has to offer – its darkest depths and its highest highs – are all present within it all the time. It's whole whether it's upside down or right-side up.' And so, it turns out, are we all.

With this new understanding of Shadow, I was finally empowered to take all of the knowledge I had about investigating hidden concepts and experiences as a writer, theatre maker and student and apply it to my own inner work.

The resilience and self-knowledge I acquired by opening myself up to my Shadow emboldened me to face my truest fears and desires head-on: I held space for the fear and imposter syndrome that kept me from my dream of writing books, and now I've written several. I started my own business after a lifetime of believing that my scattered brain couldn't handle it, and that no one would want what I was selling anyway. I confronted my loneliness while navigating a move to another country.

Eventually, I became a certified Shadow Work practitioner, and formally introduced elements of Shadow exploration into my tarot work and my writing – including an entire chapter on Shadow and the Tarot in my first book, *The Tarot Spreads Yearbook*.[1]

It was – and still is – scary to pull back the curtain and look at all the parts of myself that I had hidden away for so long, but embracing my Shadow frees me to become more fully myself every day.

I hope this book, and its gentle approach to finding your own personal way of thinking about, and relating to, your Shadow, will be a guiding light for you to see yourself, and your potential, more clearly, too.

WHAT IS SHADOW WORK?

'Shadow Work' is a widely used term for the act of intentionally engaging your Shadow in order to better understand and benefit from the knowledge and potential that lies hidden in your unconscious mind. It is intended to help you recognize and claim pieces of yourself that you may have previously been ashamed or afraid of, so that you can show yourself the acceptance, love and respect that every part of you deserves.

This work is important, not only because it helps you practise more self-compassion, but also more self-awareness and self-control. When you do the work of witnessing yourself, even the parts you'd rather not see, you can more effectively accommodate your needs and play to your strengths. Acknowledging and learning to accept all the parts of you, even if you find them 'unsavoury' is a crucial way to build trust with yourself, and when you trust yourself, you can shed the fear of everything you don't know, or don't feel you can control.

Shadow Work is not a one-size-fits-all or a one-and-done process. It looks different for everyone: it might involve journalling, artmaking, meditation, therapy, spiritual counselling, somatic work or any and all – or even none – of the above.

WHAT IS SHADOW PLAY?

Shadow Work draws us, sometimes trembling, into the unknown, but it's simply untrue that exploring your Shadow is fated to be traumatic, difficult or scary all of the time.

I have made a designated effort to temper Shadow Work with Shadow *Play*, because while it's important to take your Shadow seriously, it's equally crucial to give your Shadow something worth coming out of hiding for. And that means offering it play, joy and levity.

At its heart, engaging with your Shadow is a creative endeavour. Take it from Carl Jung himself, who said that the creative process activates the unconscious, making it 'possible for us to find our way back to the deepest springs of life'[2]. This book is imagined with the creative process in mind, because to invite our Shadow to play is to show it love. And to show our Shadow love is to bring our truest selves into the light.

Just as a sliver of light illuminates what's hidden out of sight, a sliver of play can bring clarity, discovery and comfort in the darkness. It can give us the confidence to keep going, and it can draw us deeper into the 'Work'.

Ultimately, when Shadow Work and Shadow Play converge on your Shadow Path, that's where you'll find the most growth, the most potential, the most value.

HOW TO USE THIS BOOK

This book is designed as a gentle yet transformative ten-week program to help you discover your Shadow for the first time. Consider it a soft launch into a lifelong relationship with your Shadow.

In these pages, you'll equip yourself with tools, strategies and rituals for uncovering the depths of your own soul and embracing your Shadow. And beyond that, you'll be initiated onto the age-old, collective human journey of discovering what lies beneath our surfaces, and learning how our good parts and our scary parts play equal roles in making us who we are, helping us survive in this world.

Weeks One and Two will help you wade gently towards the depths within you, without pushing you too deep too fast. The exercises will focus on establishing mutual respect, trust and curiosity between you and your Shadow.

Weeks Three, Four and Five will gently but firmly push you out of your comfort zone, challenging you to confront the painful elements of your Shadow, plunge deeper into the unknown to rediscover your hidden gifts, and to ultimately embrace your Shadow as a companion, not an enemy.

Week Six will help you learn and apply coping mechanisms for validating and soothing yourself through experiences that you may previously have opted to bury in your Shadow out of shame, pain or fear.

Week Seven will help you make strides to safely let your Shadow out into the world.

Weeks Eight and Nine will guide you to look differently, and more deeply, into your Shadow, and the stories you tell yourself about it.

Finally, in **Week Ten**, you'll look forward and back, to develop a vision of how you can continue to move forward with your Shadow based on how far you've come.

And, to help you continue navigating your Shadow Path long after you've completed Week Ten, you'll find an entire year's worth of journalling prompts in the back of this book.

Each weekly chapter in this book includes:

▶ An introduction to the theme for the week which covers important context to help you understand Shadow concepts and get a feel for how you'll be working with your Shadow in the week ahead.

▶ Suggested self-care practices you can turn to as you navigate your Shadow Path.

▶ Four in-depth exercises to help you connect with your Shadow in thought-provoking and creative ways.

▶ Exercises range from making art to meditation to journalling to outdoor experiences and more, and are intentionally varied to give you a taste of the many different ways you can work with your Shadow. At the beginning of each exercise, you'll find a breakdown of materials and time required.

▶ Reflection prompts to help you process what you learned and experienced throughout the week.

Tips for Making the Most of Your Journey

Work at your own pace

While this book can be completed in ten weeks, it doesn't have to be – you can take your time.

Do the same week twice if you feel like you haven't processed everything, take breaks when it feels right and give yourself permission to discover your Shadow as slowly as you need to.

I recommend working through only one exercise per day, and taking days off in between as needed. This will give you time to process what comes up in the exercise and recover from any challenging experiences.

If this book is your very first introduction to your Shadow, it's important to work through it chronologically, since each week builds on concepts covered in past weeks.

If you have an appetite to engage with your Shadow more frequently than the four exercises provided, turn to the journalling prompts at the end of this book on any day you're not working through an exercise.

Read each chapter ahead of time

Whenever you start a new week, I highly recommend reading each chapter through in full before diving into any individual exercise. This will help you get to know what you can expect, and plan ahead for any exercises that require you to make concrete timing plans, or (on rare occasions) to purchase materials you don't have on hand.

Reading each chapter ahead of participating in the exercises will also help you identify if there are any tasks you don't feel comfortable taking part in.

Prioritize self-care

This book endeavours to make the time you spend with your Shadow as joyful and gentle as possible. But journeying into your depths in search of hidden parts of yourself is a vulnerable process, and you're bound to encounter some level of discomfort at some point. To mitigate any negative effects, it's important that you take your self-care seriously during this journey.

To help you practise healthy coping, each weekly chapter includes self-care suggestions. Use these as needed, and/or keep up your own existing self-care practices like talk therapy, yoga, and time with loved ones throughout this journey.

Respect your mental and emotional safety

Hand-in-hand with prioritizing your self-care is respecting your own sense of mental and emotional safety throughout this process. I offer two key pieces of advice to help do this:

Don't engage with your Shadow while under the influences of alcohol or other mind-altering substances. Shadow Work and Play make you vulnerable, and substances may have adverse effects on your experience.

Take your mental health seriously – this book is not a replacement for professional mental health services, so if you think you could benefit from the support of a therapist or counsellor at any point along your journey, don't hesitate to seek out the help you need.

Focus on what resonates with you, and leave the rest behind

I encourage you to try every exercise in this book, but I don't expect you to carry every tip, tactic or suggestion I offer into your personal Shadow practice long term.

If something doesn't work for you, give yourself permission to leave it behind.

This book is a map, not a highway. We won't all get to our depths in exactly the same way, but I hope that within these pages you'll find oases of support that you can return to again and again as you need.

Use your imagination

There are no right or wrong answers when it comes to Shadow exploration. Your Shadow is a part of you, and the way that you learn to speak to it, express it and conceptualize it will be completely unique to you.

Throughout the exercises in this book, you'll regularly be prompted to imagine what your Shadow might do, say or feel. These prompts are not a test – they're an opportunity to get curious about whatever comes up for you. Give your imagination permission to conjure these answers – trust that even when you feel lost, your most intuitive response will be exactly the breadcrumb you need to keep you moving along your Shadow Path.

Document the journey for yourself

Shadow exploration is an exercise in personal evolution, so keep a record of what happens for you on this journey so that you can look back on it and chart your progress. See below for advice on maintaining a Shadow Journal.

Document the journey, first for yourself, and then catch others up later, when you can provide more context and perspective. I recommend being selective about how much you share publicly about your journey in the early stages, but I'd love to see you share photos of this book on social media (tag me @pipcardstarot).

ASSEMBLE A SHADOW PATH TOOL KIT

Before you set off on your Shadow Path, there are a few things you'll need:

A journal and something to write with

Throughout this book, you'll be prompted to record your thoughts, feelings and experiences in your journal.

Where possible, your journal should be paper – some prompts in this book invite you to mix mediums, so being able to paint/paste/manipulate the paper is important. But if you prefer to use an app on your phone, or even voice notes or video logging, do what feels right for you. If using an app, just make sure you have paper and analogue supplies for mixed media exercises.

I recommend an **unlined notebook** so that you're free to express yourself fully, not just through words, but through scribbles and doodles, mind maps, collaging and anything else you're drawn to.

A timer

Each exercise in the book includes a recommended amount of time to spend on it. While these timeframes are only suggestions that you are free to take or leave depending on what feels right for you, it is important to give yourself some kind of time boundary for the exercises. Time boundaries will help you give each exercise the time it deserves, and also ensure you don't get carried away and become overwhelmed.

You can use the timer on your phone or other device, or any manual timer.

Art supplies

We've established that engaging with your Shadow can be playful and creative, and so you're invited to get crafty and artistic throughout the course of this book.

I recommend having at minimum some **coloured pencils, crayons, markers and/or watercolours** at your disposal so that you can get colourful in your journal.

If it's fun for you, feel free to build out a more robust arts and crafts kit that you – and your Shadow – will love playing with.

Suggested additional items
- Craft or construction paper
- Collage materials (magazines, newspaper, scissors and glue)
- Clay
- Beads and wire
- Glitter
- Oil paints and canvas
- Embroidery or needlepoint materials
- Make-up
- Musical instruments

Divination tools

A tarot or oracle deck, pendulum or rune stones are optional, but can be helpful for exercises in the latter half of the book.

Take care not to rush to use them before you're invited to in the context of an exercise. While these tools can help deepen your Shadow exploration, it's important to first establish a foundational connection with your Shadow before you involve additional influence.

Candles and matches

Several exercises within this book will call for candles, so have one or two on hand. If they are scented, make sure you like the scent.

When using candles, be vigilant about safety. Ensure your candle is supported by a sturdy holder, that it's only lit in an open space and that there is no paper, fabric or other flammable material in the vicinity of the flame. Never light a candle that could be within reach of a child or pet, always let other people in your household know that you'll be lighting a candle, and never leave a candle unattended. It's also responsible to have the number for your local fire department saved in your phone, just in case.

If you have any reservations about candle safety, err on the side of caution, and opt not to use them.

DISCOVER YOUR SHADOW
TO DISCOVER YOURSELF

This book is here to help you find the courage to meet your Shadow and recognize that it's so much more than the dark parts of you that you bury.

Yes, along this journey into your Shadow you may discover uncomfortable things: memories of a heartbreak you couldn't cope with at the time, your fear of failure or your self-consciousness. But tucked up alongside these might be faith in love, the dreams you had before you felt trapped on the career ladder, the freedom of laughing without worrying about being judged, the potential for living a brave and beautiful life. You deserve to get all of those treasures back, and to learn how you can manage the painful things you experience without losing beautiful parts of yourself in the process.

In discovering your Shadow, you're going to begin the work of discovering and honouring your truest, fullest self.

Engaging with your Shadow will change your life. There's no way of knowing how until you dive in, because you can't know what you've buried until you've found it. But here are a few examples of the kind of transformations possible:

▶ A primary school teacher's Shadow journey leads her to reconnect to her dreams of becoming an actress. She'd given up on the dream after a former partner shamed her for participating in romantic scenes with other people. Reconnecting with her true creative desires and her bodily autonomy through Shadow Work and Play reignites her pursuit of the stage. She'll star in her first short film next year.

▶ After a decade of job-hopping, a clever and driven but insecure designer confronts their Shadow and realizes that their pattern of working jobs where they are taken advantage of is rooted in their upbringing, which taught them to respect authority at all costs and to value financial security over emotional safety. The act of Shadow Play and exploration help them to dream up a business that plays to their strengths.

▶ An expectant new father begins to investigate his Shadow with a counsellor. Combined with his experience supporting his partner through her pregnancy, Shadow Work helps him to reconnect to a calling for care work that he abandoned when, as a pre-teen he was repeatedly deemed 'too sensi-tive'. He's now a stay-at-home father, and plans to retrain as a nurse when his son starts school.

▶ The 'quiet' one in a friend group is tired of being overlooked – she fears she's boring, with nothing to contribute. But along her Shadow journey, she real-izes that she is, in fact, full of opinions and ideas and possesses a rich inner life that she's simply forgotten to enjoy. She recognizes that her friend group's disinterest in her life is in part due to her self-consciousness about showing up as her full self, but also in part due to their lack of appreciation for and interest in her. Shadow Work also helps her rekindle a love for reading, a passion her friends don't share.

Opening themselves up to the wells of possibility within their depths through Shadow Work and Play guided each of these people to a life that feels more authentically their own.

By questioning what was within them, they took the brave first step to dig into unknown territory – their own fears, insecurities and hang-ups, but also their lost desires, pleasures and strengths. Equipped with that knowledge, each of them was able to make more informed decisions about what would make them feel fulfilled and invigorated in their lives. They unlocked the hidden potential inside themselves and used what they found to light their paths.

Your own path to discovering your hidden depths, illuminating your potential and changing your life starts now. Think of your Shadow as the undiscovered country of yourself, the other side of your inner world, populated by all the things you don't know about yourself, but that you can grow from by seeking out and understanding.

This book is a guide for making the journey to that wild territory, a compass to help you follow your own feet on a path into the dark. All you have to do is trust that as your eyes adjust, you'll find wonders that make the work worthwhile.

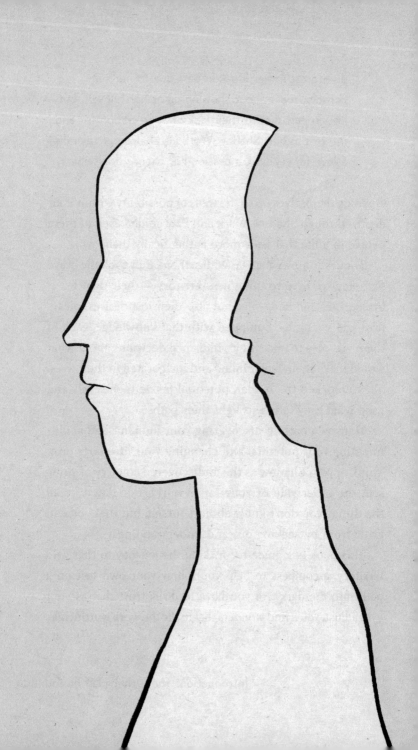

WEEK ONE:
MEET YOUR SHADOW

*This week, you'll gently explore
the concept of Shadow and take the
first step to recognizing how Shadow
manifests in your life.*

Y ou're here because you want to cultivate a deeper understanding of yourself through Shadow Work. But before you can dive in fully, you need to test the waters. To dip your toe in and gauge the temperature.

You need to meet your Shadow.

Think about it like making a new friend: you wouldn't book a week-long holiday with someone you just ran into on the street. You're going to take the time to get to know them first.

When you begin a new friendship, you go on coffee dates, you exchange texts and phone calls, you invite each other over for dinner and often meet other people in each of your networks. You see each other through many lenses. You take the time to observe one another and grow comfortable. Through your journey towards a deeper bond, you develop a sense of respect for each other's needs and boundaries in friendship; you pull back the layers of your lives piece by piece as you grow closer.

At first, it may feel frustrating to start in the shallows, to meet your Shadow as a stranger – after all, your Shadow is part of you, and your goal over the next ten weeks spent with this book is to dive deeper into your own furthest reaches. So, if thinking of your Shadow as a new friend you have to build a connection with from scratch doesn't sit well with you, imagine instead that your Shadow is a twin from whom you've been separated at birth.

Yes, you have a special, sacred bond, the depths of which are quite possibly unfathomable. Your Shadow was born alongside you – it's part of you.

But the truth is, you're still starting from very close to zero.

You may have found your twin, but you are also meeting a stranger, someone with their own set of experiences and a story you don't know anything about yet. Someone who may know just as little of your life story. Someone who you are in no position to make assumptions about, and who you probably wouldn't appreciate making assumptions about you.

So, you have to get to know each other. You have to move through the journey from being strangers to becoming close. You have to discover each other's needs, boundaries, strengths and weaknesses, in the same way you would with any new acquaintance. The possibilities for mutual understanding, for healing and growth may be deeper, based on the bond you were born into, but the process of accessing those depths is the same as when cultivating a friendship: you have to put in the time, and you have to put it in with the utmost patience and respect for the other.

This week, you'll begin the process of patiently building a foundation of respect with your Shadow, so that the deep-diving work you do together throughout the next ten weeks has a shared and safe starting point. You're going to ask your Shadow some basic questions and allow it to reveal important elements of itself to you, like its name and some of its favourite things. You're going to take the first steps towards understanding how shadow manifests in your life, and how you relate to it.

The more you lean into learning about your Shadow like a new friend, or a lost twin, the stronger the trust can be between you as you go deeper, and the more impactful the discoveries you make together will be.

SHADOW SELF-CARE FOR WEEK ONE

The following prompts and exercises for meeting your Shadow are designed to be gentle. Ruffling the feathers of your inner life can be overwhelming – even when we take it slow, so come to this week prepared with some self-care practices that you can turn to while you take these first steps towards the depth of your soul.

Week One self-care prompts

▶ Have a cup of your favourite herbal tea (or other non-caffeinated hot drink) on hand for comfort while you meet your Shadow.

▶ Plan at least one outing or activity this week that makes you feel light and playful.

▶ Book in a phone call with a friend or loved one for after one of your Shadow sessions. You don't have to discuss your Shadow experiences; instead focus on simply enjoying their company.

EXERCISE ONE: GIVE SHAPE TO YOUR SHADOW

In this meditative visualization exercise, you'll imagine laying eyes on your Shadow, and reflect on how it appears to you.

You will need
- A quiet, peaceful place where you can sit or lie down undisturbed
- A timer
- 20 minutes of your time
- Your journal and something to write with

Start by reading through the following visualization journey before closing your eyes and trying it for yourself. You don't need to memorize the entire journey, simply read through to get an idea of what's to come, and then lead yourself through the major points, staying open to where your own mind and soul lead you. If you're more comfortable following the script exactly, you can journal your way through this exercise instead of doing it with your eyes closed.

Set the timer for 10–20 minutes, whatever's most comfortable for you.

Now, are you ready to take the first step towards meeting your Shadow?

Take a journey through visualization

Allow your eyes to drift over the room that you're in and take in the space around you. Notice the interplay of shadow and light. Is the light warm or cold? Natural or artificial? Where do you notice shadows in the room? What shape and qualities do these shadows take on? How do you feel when drawing your attention to them?

Take in every shadow you can see in the room. Trace its outline with your eyes, notice the depth of its darkness and how its shape mirrors and differs from the objects casting it.

When you're ready, allow your eyes to close.

Imagine yourself in a quiet, but public place. A library, perhaps or a courtyard or a park. It's not empty here, but it's not bustling: a few people are milling around, doing their own thing. You might exchange smiles if you pass each other, but otherwise you're all content in companionable silence.

Take in the scene before you in the same way you observed your room before you closed your eyes. Notice the light in this place. What kinds of objects, architecture, flora and fauna does it illuminate? Where do you see pools of shadow, and what elements of the scene are these shadows attached to?

Take in every shadow you can see in this imagined place. Trace its outline with your eyes; notice the depth of its darkness, and how its shape mirrors and differs from the objects casting it.

Now, imagine that at a distance, some living thing –

human or animal – crosses your field of vision and draws your attention away from your task of tracing shadows.

What do you see?

Observe this being from where you are. Notice everything you can. How tall do they stand? How do they carry themselves? Are they clothed, or otherwise decorated? Are they still or on the move? Do they appear graceful or bumbling? How are they interacting with this place? How does the light catch them, and what is the quality of the shadow they cast?

Think back to the moment they first caught your attention: what detail, or action, drew your eye to them?

Imagine, now, for a split second, from across the divide between you, that this being's eyes raise to meet yours – briefly – before they move, and carry on out of your field of vision.

Let yourself watch them go.

Return your attention to the place where you are – that courtyard, library or park. To the objects and shadows you traced moments ago. Trace them again now and consider how you feel after this short encounter – your first glimpse of your own Shadow.

Let the vision of this imagined place start to fall away, object by object, shadow by shadow, until you're in the quiet dark of your own mind.

Allow your eyes to open.

Now, set your timer for another 10 minutes, reach for your journal and record what you saw. Try not to embellish or add, simply report:

- ▶ What shape did your Shadow take? Was it human, animal, something fantastic?
- ▶ What energy did your Shadow project?
- ▶ What stood out to you, physically, about your Shadow?
- ▶ How did you feel, watching it from a distance?
- ▶ What else did you experience?
- ▶ Can you sketch out some version of what you saw?

Shadow at first sight

Today, you've caught your first glimpse of your Shadow. You've seen its shape, and it has acknowledged your presence. Trust that that's enough for now.

Don't push yourself to move beyond the initial interaction you had with your Shadow within the visualization. It's not time to meet them again, or to strike up a conversation just yet. Instead, give yourself time to digest what you've learned today. To reflect on what you've seen, how you feel about it and what questions you may want to ask your Shadow when the time comes.

Before you move on with your day, consider taking a moment to practise one or more of the Week One Shadow Self-Care tips on p. 29.

When you feel ready, return to this book for the next step on your Shadow Path.

EXERCISE TWO: NAME YOUR SHADOW

In this journalling exercise, you'll gain new understanding of, and familiarity with, your Shadow by granting it a name.

Names carry knowledge and power. Consider the many roles that names play in your everyday life:

- ▶ Names help you organize your contacts and reach out to the right people when you need them.
- ▶ Names help you find the things you need – from books at the library to products on shelves to important files on your computer.
- ▶ Names help you claim the people and animals in your life. There's something sacred about naming children and pets, something intimate about nick-naming a friend.
- ▶ Names can be art in and of themselves. The titles of paintings, poems and novels give so much insight into the work in just a handful of words. The names of artists become synonymous with their work.
- ▶ Names carry history. They tell us stories about who we've come from, and who we've become.
- ▶ Names can grant access. Being connected to certain names, through family or association, can open up spaces, communities and opportunities.

- Names can be exclusive, too. They can be used in prejudice, to shame and embarrass, to judge and belittle.
- Names can be freeing. When you give yourself permission to call yourself by a name that expresses who you know yourself to be, you claim power, independence, autonomy.

You will need
- A quiet, peaceful place where you can write in private
- A timer
- 30 minutes of your time
- Your journal and something to write with

Explore names to find what you might call your Shadow

Set your timer for 5 minutes and write about your personal experience with names in your journal.

- Names that have been given to you
- Names that you have given yourself
- Names you've given to others
- Names that are special to you

Now, set the timer for another 5 minutes and ask yourself:

▶ What names have I embraced in my life?
▶ What names have I rejected?
▶ What names would I like to claim, or reclaim?

Take a moment to reflect back on Exercise One (p. 30), in which you visualized meeting your Shadow.

Close your eyes, and take yourself back to what you saw, or reflect back on what you wrote in your journal.

Then, set your timer for 20 minutes and make a list of all the names that might belong to your Shadow, given what you know at this point.

Apply no filter. No name is too silly, too grand, or even too mean.

Fully give yourself over to brainstorm and imagination: the question isn't 'What is my Shadow's definitive name?' but instead: 'What might my Shadow's name be?'

Make possibilities – not answers – your goal. Explore names that bring you joy, names that strike fear into your heart, names that remind you of someone or something, names that make you laugh and names that make you cringe, names you've never heard of, names that feel commonplace . . . any name that drops into your mind deserves a spot on the list.

Read back over the list of names you've generated.

Pay attention to which names feel empowering versus which names make a villain of your Shadow. Circle the name that you like best. Trust your intuition to tell you what 'best' is.

Maybe there's a name that makes you smile. A name that makes you feel powerful. A name that speaks to a myth or legend you feel connected to. Focus on choosing names for your Shadow that just feel right, or at the very least, make you curious.

As you move through this book for the next ten weeks, experiment with calling your Shadow by some of these names.

Giving your Shadow a name, or names, can do several important things for you on your journey into your depths:

▶ Naming your Shadow can prompt you to take ownership of your Shadow. To recognize and claim it as part of yourself. Something unique to you, something you can name.
▶ Giving your Shadow a new name can help shed some of the 'dark', 'scary' associations that come with the word 'Shadow' – calling it by something else, something you choose yourself, can help you recognize that your Shadow is so much more than the buried trauma or evil impulses that society associates with the Shadow.
▶ Naming gives you a shorthand to skirt the overwhelm that can come with confronting such a complex and boundless idea.

Keep in mind that while naming your Shadow will be a useful tool for conceptualizing its vast, hard-to-pin-down nature, and may help you feel more comfortable working with it, naming your Shadow is a creative exercise, not a genie-in-the-lamp solution. You won't suddenly become your Shadow's ruling master simply by giving it a name, and that shouldn't be your goal anyway. Remember, your Shadow is a well of possibility – to know it is a gift, not a burden. To name your Shadow is to claim it as a special friend.

Remember, too, that you yourself might go by many names in your lifetime – birth names, married names, nicknames, professional names, parental names, social media handles. Give your Shadow the same opportunity for reinvention and complex identity that you allow yourself – play with allowing it to be known by different names in different contexts.

Note: For the rest of this book, I'll continue to refer to your Shadow as, well, your Shadow – but feel encouraged to continue to play with the names you've chosen or even new names that reveal themselves to you, as you continue on your Shadow Path.

Wherefore art thou, Shadow?

Shakespeare's Juliet wasn't talking about her Shadow self when she said 'What's in a name? That which we call a rose, by any other word would smell as sweet', but her words are wisdom worth applying to your progress along the Shadow Path today.

As you bring this exercise to a close and prepare to resurface from your depths, take a moment to reflect on the positive experiences you've had so far at the early stage in your journey. Your Shadow, or whatever you decide you'd like to call it, has its own sweetness, and learning to taste it is one of the most important early steps towards integrating your Shadow and mastering your own inner depths.

Make a note of the positive experiences that come to mind, and plan to start your next Shadow session by reminding yourself of the sweetness your Shadow has to offer.

Before you move on with your day, consider taking a moment to practise one or more of the Week One Shadow Self-Care tips on p. 29.

When you feel ready, return to this book for the next step on your Shadow Path.

EXERCISE THREE: SHADOW TALISMAN

In this exercise, you'll imbue a pocket-sized object with the essence of your Shadow to help you anchor your Shadow exploration in your physical, everyday experience.

You've given your Shadow a shape and a name, and now it's time to give it some weight by creating a talisman to represent it in the physical world.

Talismans are relics that have been used in many spiritual traditions around the world for thousands of years. In a nutshell, a talisman is any object that a person imbues with special power or meaning. Lucky coins and rabbits' feet, Evil Eye amulets, crosses, horseshoes, rosary beads – all of these objects and more are examples of things that have been elevated to talisman status because of the power granted to them by the believer who carries them.

One common talisman you'll be familiar with is a wedding ring. A wedding band is a physical object that we imbue with powerful meaning: it signifies love and commitment. Partners exchange these tokens ceremonially, through rites that elevate the rings from pieces of jewellery to powerful symbols of the bigger concept they represent.

Note that the physical symbol gives weight to the idea, but it doesn't define it. Love and commitment still exist within us when we take a wedding ring off when cooking or getting it cleaned, for instance.

We don't *require* the item in order to access the power it holds but giving physical weight to an idea can be a powerful and meaningful tool for conceptualizing and representing abstract concepts.

With all this in mind, today you're going to choose a talisman that represents your Shadow.

You will need
- An object to be your Shadow Talisman
- At least 20 minutes of your time
- Your journal and something to write with

Choose your Shadow Talisman

You can source your Shadow Talisman from a second-hand shop, a walk in nature or even a browse through things you already own. If you have clay, you could even fashion something wholly new.

It might be tempting – especially this early on your Shadow Path – to invest in an expensive or grandiose item, but I recommend keeping it small, simple and cheap or free. Any object that is sturdy, pocket-sized and that appeals to you will make for the perfect Shadow Talisman.

Avoid choosing anything fragile, or any item that already holds significant meaning for you, like a family heirloom you associate with a specific relative, a souvenir from a memorable trip or a heartfelt gift from a friend.

For my own Shadow Talisman, I chose a paperweight in the form of a sleeping cat – an object that's been quietly hiding out on my desk for years. It's made of durable glass, fits neatly in the palm of my hand and immediately felt like the right choice when I first tried this exercise for myself. Other items that might make great shadow talismans include: seashells, ethically sourced crystals, inexpensive or second-hand jewellery, acorns, guitar picks or dice.

Once you've chosen your talisman, hold it against your heart and call it by the name you gave your Shadow in the last exercise. Place it in a prominent space where you can see it, and hold it in your hands, even carry it around in your pocket regularly. Write about how and why you chose your talisman in your journal.

Each time you open this book, and/or your Shadow Journal, take a moment to hold your talisman in your hands, and have it near you as you engage with your Shadow through the exercises in this book. Being in regular contact with your talisman will help you get used to the idea of your Shadow as an intrinsic ingredient in your life, rather than a scary thing to be avoided.

And if you lose it? Don't beat yourself up. Acknowledge the loss and forgive yourself. Then, choose a new talisman to work with instead. Remember: the talisman is not your Shadow, it's just a tool you're using to *represent* your Shadow. Your Shadow is inside you, part of you. You *can't* lose it. Remind yourself, and your Shadow, of this often.

Shadow favour

I like to think of Shadow Talismans like the favours women used to bestow on knights in the medieval romances. In stories, a knight might go out on a quest in service of a noble household. The lady of the house might give the knight a handkerchief or other item to carry with him on his quest, to spur him forward on his mission, but also to remind him of the welcome that awaits him on his return.

You can imagine that your talisman is a similar favour from your Shadow – something to remind you where you're coming from and where you're going, even when you feel lost in your pursuit of it.

Before you move on with your day, consider taking a moment to practise one or more of the Week One Shadow Self-Care tips on p. 29.

When you feel ready, return to this book for the next step on your Shadow Path.

EXERCISE FOUR: SHADOW SOUNDTRACK

In this creative exercise, you'll reflect on the songs that speak to your depths and connect to your Shadow through music.

Music is a deeply personal, emotive component to our lives. We play certain songs when we feel upbeat or want to improve our mood, and other songs when we feel low and don't want to be alone with that feeling. We task our personal soundtrack with helping us get through the things that bore us and the things that scare us. We painstakingly compile playlists as monuments to particular moments – even whole eras – of our lives, people we love and people we hate.

Recall the teenage romance of making a mix, the intimacy of sharing headphones, sending a playlist saying, 'Here: I made this for you, I want you to know me, and I think I know you.'

Music can be an offering. An invitation. An opening for connection. A bid at reconnection to ourselves – to our big feelings. To deep emotions – love, hurt, anger, desire, that we often tie stones to and submerge as we get older. Feelings that sink and wait for us to find them again. Feelings that animate our Shadows.

Music is the medium that, according to prolific fairy-tale writer Hans Christian Anderson, speaks where words fail. Words are not always capable of capturing the recesses of our souls, the unconscious space where Shadow lives. But music echoes in the depths, speaking to all of the hidden parts of ourselves and creating harmony where we once thought there would only be discord.

With that in mind, your task now is to curate a musical offering to your Shadow. One that opens up a line of shared connection that speaks directly to the feelings that animate your Shadow – and you. Think of it as a mix-tape for your Shadow. A musical love-letter that says here: I made this for you, I want you to know me, and I think I know you.

You will need
- A private place
- A device where you can play and save music tracks
- Speakers and/or headphones
- At least an hour of your time
- Your journal and something to write with

Take your time over the next several days to reflect in your journal about songs or other musical pieces that move you on a deep level. Consider what they tell you about your unconscious desires, fears, and wounds. Choose tracks too, that reconnect you with joyful experiences you haven't reconnected with in years. Take the time to listen through each piece or song, maybe even more than once, and reflect on how it feels to listen to it. What does each track bring up for you, and how do you feel in your body when you listen? What moments within each track make you feel most connected to your own depths?

Curate a playlist of at least ten tracks, and write liner notes to explain the choices on your mix to your Shadow. Tell it how the track reminds you of what you may have buried within your depths, of what you want to explore within your depths, and of the warm feelings you want to extend to your Shadow.

Where words fail, Shadow speaks

As you move along your Shadow Path, let this mix become the soundtrack to your journey. Listen to it regularly and continue to add to it as you discover new songs or pieces relevant to your experience, and as you peel back the layers of your Shadow and discover new dimensions to your own depths.

Before you move on with your day, consider taking a moment to practise one or more of the Week One Shadow Self-Care tips on p. 29.

When you feel ready, return to this book for the next step on your Shadow Path.

Week One Reflection Prompts

This week you've taken the first steps on your Shadow Path: you've made initial contact with your Shadow and started to get acquainted with it by learning its name, giving it weight and form and connecting to it through music.

Now, as your first week comes to a close, set your timer for 15 minutes and reflect back on the week in your journal.

Ask yourself
- What did I discover about my Shadow this week?
- Which exercise from this week taught me the most?
- Which exercise from this week was the most joyful?
- What support and comfort could I benefit from before heading into the next week?

WEEK TWO:
STUDY YOUR SHADOW

This week, you'll build on what you learned last week and take a closer look at your Shadow, becoming an ambitious student of the qualities and patterns that are hiding beneath your surface.

When we discover new passions in our lives – people, hobbies, places or ideas – the first thing we tend to do is go on a quest for more knowledge about those passions. We become star students of the objects that hold our attention.

We discover a musician's work that speaks to us, and so we enthusiastically learn all their lyrics and lore; we scour museums and libraries to learn about an era of history that fascinates us; we seek out every recommendation we can to help us travel like locals in our ideal holiday spots; we learn all of our new crush's favourite foods, songs and places; we study the habits and moods of our children and pets so that we can adjust to them. We are all in constant pursuit of knowledge about what interests us.

But of course, like all things, a thirst for knowledge has a Shadow side. Our minds aren't only piqued by things we find delightful. The imagination can be equally captivated by things that frighten, unsettle and even disgust us.

In some cases, we find our desire for discovery dwarfed

by fear of what we may discover – about the world, and about ourselves. In other cases, our studiousness is doused out by shame – our interest may be deemed nosy or otherwise inappropriate.

To survive, we learn to conceal our natural curiosity – first from others, and then, often, from ourselves. We lose touch with our wild thirst for knowledge, becoming protective of what we already know, what is already comfortable. We convince ourselves that our small lives are enough, that there's nothing else out there, or that whatever else *is* out there, it is too dangerous, too dark to pursue, that we are too fragile to venture into it.

Your Shadow Path is, above all things, a reclamation of your curiosity, an acknowledgement of your desire – and courage – to discover the unknowable, and a commitment to learning about yourself, even when the material becomes challenging, unflattering or scary.

To take this next step on your path, you are going to become a student of your own Shadow. That means you're going to build on the foundations you put into place in Week One – that gentle work you did to coax your Shadow into the light – and you're going to take a better look at it.

You'll have the opportunity to identify patterns and themes present in your Shadow, and your relationship with it, by paying attention to your dreams. You'll get to ask your Shadow the questions you're most desperate – and perhaps most afraid – to ask of it. You'll trace a map of your Shadow, the better to chart the path into your depths. And you'll learn to step back and interpret your Shadow like a prized work of art.

Throughout this week, you'll be shifted outside of your comfort zone, prompted to study your Shadow closely and deepen your understanding of what it means to be on your Shadow Path.

Don't rush to become an expert. As a student of your Shadow, you're here to be a keen observer, to respect that you still have a lot to learn before you become an esteemed scholar of your own depths and to slowly, meticulously apply your curiosity so that you can learn everything you can about your Shadow.

As you practise drawing your curiosity out of from where it's been buried in your Shadow, think of this week as a masterclass in giving yourself permission to ask questions. A course in daring to use your imagination. And an exercise in revealing your Shadow itself, through thoughtful and attentive study.

SHADOW SELF-CARE FOR WEEK TWO

This week's prompts and exercises are designed to help you observe and better understand your Shadow without feeling like you have to jump into the deep end just yet. Still, the very act of observing your Shadow can be a confronting, sometimes disorienting experience, so it's important to ensure that you're proactive when it comes to caring for your mental and emotional health. Come to this week prepared with some self-care practices that you can turn to while you immerse yourself in studying your Shadow.

Week Two self-care prompts

▶ Take time to get some fresh air before and after the time you spend with this book. It can be as simple as stepping out of your front door and feeling the earth beneath your feet for a couple of breaths. Walks with loved ones (human or animal) are encouraged.

▶ Practise good sleep hygiene. This week, you'll be encouraged to reflect on your dreams, which may disrupt your regular sleeping habits. For that reason, it's particularly important to make sure you: don't consume too much caffeine; take the time to wind down before bed; practise a calming wake-up routine such as a short yoga or breathwork session in the mornings if possible.

▶ Write a note of encouragement to your future self
and keep it nearby for when you need a pick-me-up
later.

EXERCISE ONE: SHADOW DREAMING

In this journalling exercise, you'll practise recognizing how your Shadow communicates to you through dreams.

Dreams have been considered keys to our unconscious depths for millennia, long before modern psychoanalysis claimed the interpretation of dreams as a method of uncovering what's buried within our psyches.

Ancient religions believed dreams were messages from the gods and nightmares a source of demonic torture. Shamans from many cultures have long sought out dream-states as channels for spiritual wisdom, while wise men and women around the world have helped people unknot the stories and secrets of their dreams so they could make sense of their waking lives.

Carl Jung, the father of contemporary theories around Shadow Work, confirmed as much in his 1917 essay 'On the Psychology of the Unconscious'. Jung acknowledges how the dream was in ancient times 'a harbinger of fate, a portent and comforter, a messenger of the gods.' Jung goes on to say that in modern times, 'we see it [the dream] as the emissary of the unconscious, whose task it is to reveal the secrets that are hidden from the conscious mind, and this it does with astounding completeness.'[3]

In other words, Shadow and the dreaming world have

always been intertwined – and for good reason. Our dreams can be portals into our depths.

> You will need
> - 10–15 minutes when you go to bed every day this week and 10–15 minutes when you wake up
> - Your journal and something to write with

This week, your task is to study your dreams and draw out the knowledge your Shadow is sharing with you as you sleep. That means opening yourself up to the possibility that your depths are not buried quite so deep that they're unreachable. That in drifting off to sleep, you're taking a meaningful step towards communicating with your Shadow. That every night's sleep is an opportunity to understand yourself better.

Before you get started, a gentle warning: it's best to avoid thinking of your dreams as literal messages from your Shadow, predictions for your future or repressed memories. Identifying that kind of nuanced wisdom is a journey you can consider setting off on only once your Shadow Path is well trodden, and you feel that you and your Shadow speak the same language fluently. For now, think of the fragments of your dreams that follow you into the waking world as impressions, clues or breadcrumbs leading you closer to what lies in your depths.

How to recognize your Shadow's communications through dreams

Step one: each night, before you go to sleep, take some time to prime yourself to receive messages from your Shadow while you sleep. Here are a few ways you might do this:

▶ Reflect on a moment in your day when you felt aware of your Shadow.

▶ Listen to a track or two from the Shadow Soundtrack you curated in Week One.

▶ Lie down in bed with the lights off, ready to go to sleep. Close your eyes and take several deep breaths before allowing yourself to settle into your natural breathing rhythm. Imagine yourself on a shoreline, and with each breath take a step deeper into the water, until you are completely submerged. Let the water carry you, in time with the rhythm of your breath, off to sleep.

Step two: each morning when you wake up, immediately and before you get out of bed, take 5 minutes to record your dreams in your Shadow Journal. You might do this by sketching or describing particularly potent images or sensations you experienced, or by making a bulleted list of everything you can remember, or in another way that feels right for you, because there's no wrong way to record your dreams. Record good dreams and bad dreams – your Shadow is just as capable of sending you pleasure as it is fear or pain.

Step three: once you've recorded your dream, ask yourself this question: 'What unconscious desires, fears, urges or experiences have been brought up to me through this night's dreams?'

Reflect on your answer, and on what it tells you about your Shadow. Write down your thoughts and in the spirit of this week's theme, see whatever comes up for you as a nugget of knowledge to add to your notes as a student of your Shadow. Don't feel pressure to act on the knowledge that arises from your dreams; trust that knowing what you know is more than enough for now.

Shadow dreams are made of this

This week's exercise challenges you to cede some control to your unconsciousness by allowing your dreams to reveal elements of your Shadow to you. Tread carefully and remember your role in this phase of your Shadow Path is that of a student. Allow yourself to focus on observing and learning.

Consider continuing your dream journalling beyond the week-long exercise. As you get to know your Shadow better over the course of your journey along the Shadow Path, you'll feel more fluent with the impressions your Shadow sends you through dreams, and your dreams will start to feel less like an overpacked rummage sale you have to wade through, and more like a compass, guiding you in the direction of more coherent communication with your Shadow.

Before you move on with your day, consider taking a moment to practise one or more of the Week Two Shadow Self-Care tips on p. 53.

When you feel ready, return to this book for the next step on your Shadow Path.

EXERCISE TWO: SHADOW Q+A

For this journalling exercise, you'll practise getting curious with your Shadow, and challenge yourself to ask it some tough questions so that you can learn to understand it better.

The best students are curious, willing to ask questions and comfortable acknowledging the discomfort of *not* knowing, so that they can openly pursue what they wish to know.

The same can be said of a good journalist. Curiosity is king, and the dogged pursuit of knowledge and the truth is the ultimate key to a compelling, meaningful story that has the potential to change how readers understand and engage with a topic.

As a lifelong student and a former journalist, I can attest that being able to identify the 'right' questions (which sometimes means those that make us feel the most embarrassed or vulnerable) is the secret to getting the most prized information. It's true for me now, too, as a tarot reader and author. I often tell my tarot clients and students that if they aren't finding meaning in the cards they've drawn, they haven't yet asked the question that will lead them to the answer they need. Writing a book is similar: the book's premise is a question I ask myself, or that someone has asked of me. My job is to approach that question in a way that elicits a meaningful answer.

Shadow Work, too, is all about questions. It's simple to start. Call and response, a game of Marco Polo, but for the depths of your soul. You call out into the void, and all you need is confirmation that you've been heard. The question is 'Are you there?' The answer, once you allow yourself to hear it, is 'Yes'.

For your Shadow, the stakes of this game are high. For so long, you've been conditioned to bury your Shadow. To avoid investigating it. To pretend you can't hear it when it calls. To respond to its 'are you there's with even less than a 'no'. With nothing at all. Becoming a student of your Shadow means being brave enough to ask your Shadow questions.

In Week One, you opened yourself up to cues from your Shadow about its shape, its name, the music that speaks to it.

Now you're ready to ask it some direct questions.

You will need
- A quiet, peaceful place where you can work and play in private
- A timer
- 40 minutes of your time
- Your journal and something to write with

Make a list of questions to ask your Shadow

Start by setting your timer for 10 minutes and make a list of all the questions you'd like to ask your Shadow.

Your questions can range from silly (what's your favourite colour?) to serious (what has it been like for you to feel ignored by me?) to playful (what's a joyful memory you've been holding on to?) – and anywhere in between.

The only rule, for now, is to avoid any questions that direct blame or shame onto your Shadow. Remember that you're here to learn, not cast judgement.

Once your timer goes off, or you've got a healthy list going, review your questions and choose five to attempt to answer.

Set your timer for another 20–30 minutes, and spend the rest of your time imagining how, given what you know about your Shadow at this point, your Shadow might answer the five questions you've chosen. Don't pressure yourself to get these answers 'right' – trust that the intuitive answers that bubble up are what you need to write down.

Front-page Shadow

If you'd like to take this exercise even further, imagine yourself as an award-winning journalist whose editor has assigned you to write an in-depth, gushing cover story about your Shadow. Use the questions and answers you've journalled about to draft an article in the style of a celebrity profile, and thoughtfully reflect on what this project reveals about your Shadow – and about you, as the writer. Ask your Shadow follow-up questions as necessary while you write.

Remember, however, that this is a creative exercise, one that's designed to help you explore your Shadow and invite it out to play, but not a process intended to help you put your Shadow in a box. Trust that, like any front-page celebrity story, your Shadow questions and answers are only one part of a bigger story . . . there's always more you don't know, always more questions worth asking and always a different angle through which to look at your subject.

Before you move on with your day, consider taking a moment to practise one or more of the Week Two Shadow Self-Care tips on p. 53.

When you feel ready, return to this book for the next step on your Shadow Path.

EXERCISE THREE: SHADOW LANDSCAPE

In this visualization exercise you'll chart a bird's eye view of the vast expanse of your Shadow, so that you can gain some clarity about what you know and all you still have left to learn.

Are you ready to push the boundaries of what you've learned about your Shadow and discover the landscape of your own hidden depths?

Start by reading through the following visualization before closing your eyes and trying it for yourself. You don't need to memorize the entire journey; simply read it through to get a sense of the content and then lead yourself through the major points, staying open to where your own mind and soul lead you.

If you're more comfortable following the script exactly, you can journal your way through this exercise instead of doing it with your eyes closed.

You will need
- A quiet, peaceful place where you can sit or lie down without being disturbed
- A timer
- 20 minutes of your time
- Your journal and something to write with

Shadow landscape visualization

Set the timer for 10 minutes.

Begin by taking several deep breaths, focusing on the sensation of the air filling up your chest and belly. If it helps, put the tips of your fingers together and place your hands flat on your belly so you can feel it rise when you breathe in. Allow your attention to settle into the rhythm of that expansion.

When you feel ready, close your eyes and continue to notice your breathing, with your attention focused on the sensation of expansion each time you inhale.

Once you feel comfortable with the rhythm of your breath, allow your attention to expand outwards, feeling into the room you're currently in. Try, with your eyes still closed, to visualize the room. Imagine your attention tracing its anatomy, from surface to surface, corner to corner, as if you were making a map of it in your mind. Name the parts of the room and the features of its landscape as you explore.

Once you have a clear map of the room in your head, take a deep breath in. As you exhale, allow the image of the room to fall away and the vision in your mind's eye to fade to black.

It's now time to imagine another landscape . . . to craft another map. This time, you're going to map your Shadow.

So, start by taking another deep breath. Inhale deeply through the nose, and exhale slowly out of pursed lips. Turn your attention once again to the expansion of your breath in and chart the fall as you breathe out. Do this a few times, until you feel comfortable.

When you're ready, imagine yourself looking down on a village, as if you were flying over it in a hot air balloon. This village represents everything you currently know about yourself and the way you present yourself to the world. Take time to notice the familiar places – perhaps there's an attractive coffee shop on the corner that represents the qualities you're confident about, and a dark alley that stands in for the insecurities you know that you carry. There might be a stately mansion on the edge of town that represents your ambitions, and a green park that represent your healthy relationships.

Now, imagine at the edge of town a wood. It's one you've ventured into, but still find a little frightening and disorienting at night. This wood represents everything you know about your Shadow right now. Squint through the tops of the trees to glimpse your Shadow path, and notice landmarks you've already passed on your journey. A sapling might represent the moment you gave your Shadow a name; a bird's nest might mark your experience crafting a mix-tape for your Shadow.

Allow your view to broaden and begin to identify parts of the forest that represent those elements of your Shadow you've started to become familiar with. One copse of trees might symbolize the love of singing you left behind in childhood, after you felt shamed for the quality of your voice. A brook might stand in for the buried tension with a friend or parent that has been surfacing through dreams lately.

As you float over the trees, notice that the forest gives way to a shoreline, which drops into dark, deep waters. Here lies the full scope of your unconscious, the place where your Shadow lives.

Notice how far it stretches. Notice any islands and ships that float on its surface. Imagine what parts of your Shadow these might represent, what questions and explorations they prompt within you.

As you survey the huge sky and sheer scope of your depths, inhale deeply, and let the mingled flavour of salty sea air move through your lungs.

When you're ready, take one final breath and one final glimpse of your Shadow Landscape before allowing the image to fall away as you return your consciousness to the room you're in now.

Allow your eyes to open.

Map what you saw

Now, reach for your journal and sketch out a map of what you saw. Try not to embellish, add elements or worry about drawing 'well'. Simply record what you witnessed, and then reflect in your journal on the following prompts:

▶ What did it feel like to view the landscape of your Shadow from a distance?
▶ What did you learn about yourself and your Shadow through this visualization?

- What areas of the map are you curious to explore further?
- What areas of the map are you most wary to tread into?

Chart your Shadow course

Your Shadow landscape is bound to change as you journey down your Shadow Path, but now that you have a vision of the vast country you're exploring, you can begin to gain your bearings and identify what parts of the landscape feel safe and compelling for you to explore.

You can add depth to this exercise by taking the time to turn the map you sketched into art. Look to real-life maps for inspiration, and put your creativity to work to imagine an in-depth, fantasy-novel style map of your own unconscious depths. Play with colour, style and media to create a singular map that can help you chart your Shadow Path, and inspire you to explore further.

Before you move on with your day, consider taking a moment to practise one or more of the Week Two Shadow Self-Care tips on p. 53.

When you feel ready, return to this book for the next step on your Shadow Path.

EXERCISE FOUR: SHADOW GALLERY

In this field trip exercise, you'll seek out new ways of seeing, and relating to, your Shadow by studying art.

The legendary painter and sculptor Michelangelo once called art a shadow of the divine.

He wasn't intentionally referencing the Shadow as we've defined it in this book – he was speaking of spiritual beauty, of God. Still, we can adapt this idea to Shadow Work and Play. If we imagine art as the shadow of spiritual beauty, then art becomes a manifestation of the deep, unknowable truths within us – whether we are making it, or observing it. A spiritual beauty of its own kind.

You already know that creative expression is a mainstay of your Shadow Path. And so far, as you've wandered along your Shadow Path, you've leaned heavily on your own creativity to help you visualize and connect with your Shadow.

But there's more to creativity than making and expressing. Consuming art, and engaging with it, is essential for fuelling the imagination. Surveying art can also be a powerful tool for seeking out your Shadow and finding new pathways into your own depths.

Consider your past experiences with art that moves you. Photographs, paintings, films. Think of the images that have made you feel seen, wonderstruck, reverent. Reflect on the ways you've been drawn to look closer at a captivating work, to discover more about the artist, their life and the story behind the work.

In the same way that you study a work of art in order to make sense of it, and connect more deeply to it, you should approach studying your Shadow.

Engaging with art is, by its very nature, a studious act, even if you feel like the furthest thing from an art expert. You start by taking in the work. This first pass is a study in and of itself, you register what you see, make sense of it and decide if you want to investigate further. If the work compels you, you might step physically closer, or zoom in on your device.

Looking at art helps us practise the art of looking deeper – the very skill you're honing on your Shadow Path. And, when we look deeper at art, at our experience with it, we are simultaneously looking deeper into our own souls.

So today, your task is to study your Shadow through studying art. If you're able to, plan a trip to a local gallery or museum. If this isn't feasible, you can use your computer to browse the digital archives of major art institutions instead. The Metropolitan Museum of Art, Rijksmuseum and Guggenheim all allow you to browse their permanent collections online, while Google Arts and Culture houses a treasure trove of art from around the world to explore. Give yourself a little time to toggle around these sites – they curate multiple themed sections featuring different artists, mediums, movements, themes and styles, so you'll want to explore and find a curation that's interesting to you.

You will need
- Access to a local art museum or gallery, or a device with internet access
- 45+ minutes of your time (plus travel if necessary)
- Your journal and something to write with

Visit a gallery or museum

When you are at your chosen destination (or on the website if doing the exercise digitally), start by approaching one work of art and taking it in. Don't try to analyse it at first, and don't let your attention wander to the description or curator's note yet – just allow yourself to absorb what you're looking at. Let your eyes linger on the details that stand out to you. Let yourself feel whatever feelings naturally arise, even if that feeling is discomfort or boredom.

When you're ready, imagine that somewhere, concealed within the work of art you're looking at, your Shadow is hiding, looking out at you.

Consider the following

- What do I like and dislike about this work of art?
- What other feelings are coming up for me?
- How does this work of art reflect my Shadow?
- How does my Shadow feel about finding itself in this work of art?
- What element of this work is most likely to be harbouring my Shadow?
- How does this work of art challenge what I thought I knew about my Shadow?
- What does looking at this work make me curious about?

Repeat this process with as many works as you feel up to engaging with, and take breaks to note down your impressions in your journal where necessary. Take photos and sketch out the works of art that leave particular impressions on you, so that you can revisit them later.

Pay attention to the patterns that emerge as you move through the exercise. Is there a specific artist or style whose work you feel speaks to you on a deep level? Are there specific questions about your Shadow that continually crop up as you take in the art? Do you notice any recurring visual pulling you in or repelling you? How might those patterns teach you more about your Shadow?

The art of Shadow

In seeking out your Shadow through art, you may have discovered new things about your own depths, or even been inspired to create your own Shadow art. This week, keep that creative spark alive by continuing to notice where you see reflections of your Shadow in creative works beyond paintings and sculptures in a gallery.

Strive to see how your Shadow is reflected in the characters or themes of your favourite TV shows. Read poetry and look for your Shadow between the lines. Return to the Shadow mix-tape you curated last week and expand it with more tracks that artfully capture your deepening experience with your Shadow.

Keep notes in your journal and consider how finding your Shadow in art inspires you to express your Shadow experience through your own creative explorations.

As always, consider taking a moment to practise one or more of the Week Two Shadow Self-Care tips on p. 53.

When you feel ready, return to this book for the next step on your Shadow Path.

Week Two Reflection Prompts

This week you've forged further along your Shadow Path by seeking out knowledge about your Shadow and yourself. You've studied your Shadow through art, dreams, question-and-answer interviews and maps, and while it's impossible to see all the way to the bottom, you definitely have a clearer notion of your own depths than you did a week ago.

As your second week on the Shadow Path comes to a close, set your timer for 15 minutes and reflect back on the week in your journal.

Ask yourself
- What did I discover about my Shadow this week?
- Which exercise from this week taught me the most?
- Which exercise from this week was the most joyful?
- What support and comfort could I benefit from before heading into the next week?

WEEK THREE:
CONFRONT YOUR
SHADOW WOUNDS

*This week, you'll lean on the foundation
of knowledge and trust you've built with
your Shadow so far. You'll address some
of the negative elements your Shadow
brings to the table, all the while building
towards a deeper understanding and
acceptance of all that lies within you.*

Your journey on the Shadow Path so far has been about creating a sense of safety and familiarity with your Shadow. You've focused on cultivating knowledge and respect for the hidden depths within you.

You know now that there's no need to be afraid of your depths, as long as you show them the respect they deserve.

Still, there's no denying that some depths are darker and more dangerous than others. Your Shadow is vast and complex; you've seen how it can be capable of harbouring hidden beauty, potential and joy. But you know, too, that those depths also hide pain, anger and grief – things you may have buried out of sight and mind because you didn't want to – or didn't know how to – cope with facing them head-on.

Those hidden hurts are the reason that many people avoid ever setting out on a path to explore their Shadows. They double down on neglecting their Shadows, fearing the hidden darkness a journey of self-discovery might bring to the surface. They twist the narrative – casting the Shadow as an untrustworthy, villainous enemy: the source of darkness, instead of the receptacle that is assigned to hold what they would rather bury than make sense of.

It's important to remember that the things you fear are things *you've* buried, not things your Shadow has cultivated to spite you.

Confronting your Shadow, as you'll come to learn over this next week, is less about hurling blame on your unconscious and more about recognizing the mutual pain that you and your Shadow have caused one another in your bids to survive.

At this stage, you might be asking yourself: 'Is the rest of my journey down the Shadow Path going to be a harrowing reckoning with everything that's dark within me? And is the Shadow the source of that darkness, or merely the place I've forced it to live? Is it worth disrupting my life to explore the part of my psyche where I've hidden my darkest fears, desires, and shames?'

Here's the truth: what's buried is highly likely to come to the surface in some way, shape or form eventually, whether you seek it out or not. The feelings, fears and desires that you suppress want to be expressed. The Shadow can only keep all those things safe for so long before the dam breaks, and everything you thought you could hold back spews through, uncontrolled.

Confronting your Shadow will help you to see it more clearly, to understand how it operates – and why – so that you're better prepared for those moments when what is held in your depths overflows. This week's work will help you learn to keep yourself afloat and navigate the storm, instead of letting the undertow drag you down.

While you're confronting your Shadow over the next week, be open to the ways in which it may confront you back. Both of you have been lost, both of you have been hurt, both of you have acted out against the other.

SHADOW SELF-CARE FOR WEEK THREE

This week, you're doing the hard work of confronting your Shadow – and by extension, confronting yourself. This process can be uncomfortable, challenging and exhausting. As you step into this next leg of your Shadow Path, it's critical to lead with self-compassion and gentleness. If this week isn't a good time to delve into challenging material, consider taking a break or reviewing your progress so far, and planning to move ahead next week. And whenever you do feel comfortable taking the next steps, ensure you've got plans in place to give yourself a little extra care.

Week Three self-care prompts

▶ Prioritize activities that help you regulate your emotions before, after and even during your Shadow sessions this week. Make a list of what these activities might be, so you have them on hand when you need them. Here's a few to get you started: taking gentle exercise, having a hot shower, lighting a candle, closing your eyes and taking deep breaths for one minute, making a cup of tea, crafting or making art , or any other way you create peace and perspective in your life.

▶ Create a protection ritual. Your work this week may feel vulnerable. To help you get some distance from the emotional labour you're doing, consider creating a ritual of protection that you can put into practice when you're not actively doing Shadow Work, or for times of your day that you feel particularly vulnerable – like before bed. Your ritual can be simple: you might repeat a mantra for yourself, like 'I am safe, secure and well. I'm not afraid of my Shadow, and I trust myself to stay afloat.' You can also include meaningful objects that make you feel safe: light a candle that soothes you, or place a special crystal, tarot card or other meaningful object by your bedside before you sleep. If you pray, or participate in other religious practices, seek out specific rituals for protection within your religious tradition.

▶ Set aside time in your schedule, a whole day if possible, to rest, relax and take a temporary retreat from your Shadow Path and the other demands of life. Watch your favourite movies, go to your favourite places or book a massage, yoga class or other somatic experience. You're doing hard work, and you deserve to soothe yourself.

EXERCISE ONE: WANTED FOR SHADOW CRIMES

In this creative exercise, you'll create a visual aid to represent exactly what you're holding against your Shadow – and what it's holding against you.

Your Shadow is not inherently 'dark' or 'evil', but that doesn't mean that there aren't dark parts of you tucked away beneath the surface. Roses have thorns, kittens have claws and your Shadow, too, has the capacity to be both sweet and sharp.

Your Shadow Path is, at the crux, a quest to integrate those sweet and sharp parts, so that you can know, accept and love yourself more fully.

To do this, you must begin to reckon with the ways you've experienced hurt at your Shadow's hand. For example, you might feel your Shadow enables certain destructive habits or negative patterns in relationships that cause you pain. You might blame the things you've buried within it for contributing to moments in your life that you define as failures, or experiences where you felt victimized. You might feel resentful that your Shadow preserved all those things you buried within it instead of making them go away forever.

You also have to recognize the hurt you've caused your Shadow by neglecting it, leaving it to fend for itself against the least flattering parts of you, and for rejecting those parts in the first place.

In that spirit, today you're going to confront your Shadow by calling out the crimes you and your Shadow have committed against each other. You'll diffuse some of the tension by expressing the complicated experience through art.

You will need
- A quiet, peaceful place where you can work in private
- A timer
- 30–40 minutes of your time
- Art supplies, such as paper and coloured pencils, collage materials and/or design software
- Your journal and something to write with

Prepare the chargesheet

Set your timer for 5 minutes and open your journal. At the top of a new page, write down:

'I'm angry at my Shadow because . . .', then fill in the blank.

Rewrite the prompt and answer it again . . . do this as many times as you can over 5 minutes.

When the time is up, take a moment to regulate yourself: you could make a cup of tea, step outside into the sunlight, listen to a song you love.

Then, when you're ready, return to your journal and set

the time for another 5 minutes. At the top of a new page, write down:

'My Shadow is angry at me because . . .', then fill in the blank.

Rewrite the prompt and answer it again . . . do this as many times as you can over 5 minutes.

Take another break for regulation if you need it, then return to the lists you've made and review them. Identify the most serious 'crime' on each list and circle it.

Now that you've articulated some of the damage caused, it's time to break out your art supplies and design old-fashioned WANTED posters for you and your Shadow. Declare the crime committed, where each of you was last seen, what you were last seen doing and name a suitable reward if caught.

Don't be afraid to have fun with this. Yes, the hurts you and your Shadow have done to each other may be serious, but applying a playful approach to the strains on your relationship to your Shadow can help diminish tension and build understanding.

Partners in Shadow crime

Display your WANTED posters side-by-side and consider what these two outlaws have in common. In what ways have you been accomplices to each other's bad behaviour?

Reflect too, on what separates you. How have you betrayed each other and can you justify your actions against each other?

As always, consider taking a moment to practise one or more of the Week Three Shadow Self-Care tips on p. 81.

When you feel ready, return to this book for the next step on your Shadow Path.

EXERCISE TWO: SHADOW IMPACT STATEMENT

In this journalling exercise, you'll confront your Shadow head-on by itemizing the damage it has done to you. Then, you'll turn the exercise on yourself, and list the harm you've caused to your Shadow.

When someone is convicted of a crime, those whose lives have been affected by their actions are sometimes invited to speak in court to give a Victim Impact Statement that details how they were affected by the actions of the perpetrator.

A Victim Impact Statement serves three key purposes:

It can influence a judge's decision regarding the severity of the punishment that will be meted out for the crime; the statement forces the perpetrator to confront their actions head-on and recognize the extent of the harm they've caused; finally, the opportunity to deliver a statement in court gives victims a powerful method of communicating about what happened to them, and a chance to make clear how hardship they endured as a result of the perpetrator's actions impacted their wellbeing.

Though it's a raw and vulnerable experience, writing and delivering a Victim Impact Statement can be profoundly cathartic. The process can help the affected person reclaim personal agency and empowerment that is compromised through victimization and enable them to get closure on injustice they suffered.

This week, you're confronting your Shadow; by necessity, this requires reflecting on the way you've been impacted by the painful aspects of your Shadow, as well as being confronted by the impact of the pain you've caused to yourself and your Shadow through neglect and rejection.

Earlier this week, you made a list of reasons you're angry at your Shadow, reasons it might be angry at you, and identified the major crimes you've committed against each other. Now, you're going to reflect on the lasting effects of those wrongdoings and craft two Victim Impact Statements.

You will need
- A quiet, peaceful place where you can work in private
- A timer
- 30 minutes of your time
- Your journal and something to write with

Write your Impact Statements

First, you're going to directly address your Shadow and call it out on the ways it's caused you harm. Set your timer for 10 minutes and allow yourself to write freely about what you've experienced as a result of the hurts your Shadow is responsible for – think relationships that have been damaged, opportunities lost, peace you've been unable to find.

When you finish, take a few minutes away from your journal

and regulate yourself: you could cuddle a pet, take a few deep breaths or send a message to a friend to check in.

Once you feel ready, set your timer for another 10–15 minutes. This time, you're going to address yourself, from your Shadow's point of view. Write freely, from your Shadow's perspective, about what it's been like for your Shadow to be neglected and shouldered with the weight of the emotions, experiences, desires and fears you've buried.

When you're finished, take some more time to regulate yourself.

If you feel up to it, read back over the statements you've written, and thank yourself and your Shadow for the honesty, vulnerability and bravery it took to share your stories.

Holding space for Shadow

In the legal system, a Victim Impact Statement informs a perpetrator of the consequences of their crimes. But as you reflect on your statements, you'll probably notice that you and your Shadow have done plenty to punish each other already.

Instead of focusing on what you or your Shadow deserve as a result of your negative behaviours, consider how this exercise gives you a new perspective on yourself and your Shadow. Consider how you can change your behaviour towards your Shadow for the better, and how you can teach your Shadow to treat you well, too.

While you don't need to feel rushed to fully forgive your

Shadow for the real hurt it played a role in perpetuating on you (there's time for that later down the line), this can still be a turning-point in how you do – and don't – interact. Think of this exchange of impacts as the beginning of a stalemate. You don't have to reach total healing to reach an understanding.

As always, consider taking a moment to practise one or more of the Week Three Shadow Self-Care tips on p. 81.

When you feel ready, return to this book for the next step on your Shadow Path.

EXERCISE THREE: SEE YOUR SHADOW

In this meditative visualization exercise, you'll build on the last time you imagined the shape of your Shadow, in Week One. This time, you'll get beyond a fleeting glance, and connect face-to-face with your Shadow.

You will need
- A quiet, peaceful place where you can sit or lie down
- A timer
- 20 minutes of your time
- Your journal and something to write with

Start by reading through the following visualization journey before closing your eyes and trying it for yourself. You don't need to memorize the entire journey; simply read through to get a sense of the content, and then lead yourself through the major points, staying open to where your own mind and soul lead you.

If you're more comfortable following the script exactly, you can journal your way through this exercise instead of doing it with your eyes closed.

Meditative visualization

When you're ready to start, sit or lie down as you prefer then set the timer for 10 minutes.

Begin with your eyes open.

Take several deep breaths and focus on feeling present in the room that you're in – take note of what you see and hear in the space around you.

As you continue to breathe, narrow your focus down to the specific place where you are sitting or lying. Pay attention to the surface your body is in contact with, the quality of the air you're breathing in, the details of the objects closest to you. Finally, bring your focus into your own body as you allow the eyes to close.

When you feel ready, bring your mind back to that neutral, public place you imagined yourself in when you first gave shape to your Shadow at the beginning of your journey with this book. Imagine yourself there once again. Take the time to settle in, to notice the space around you in your mind's eye.

Now, imagine your Shadow wandering into the space, some distance from where you sit.

Allow yourself to look directly at it. Watch it from afar, familiarizing yourself with the way it moves – or doesn't. See within this imagined version of your Shadow everything you've come to learn about it so far – the flattering and the unsavoury.

Now, feel your Shadow looking back at you. Hold its gaze

and let yourself be seen. Sit in this recognition for as long as you can.

When you're ready, take a deep breath in, and imagine you and your Shadow each taking one step closer to one another, the better to see and understand each other. Don't cringe away from the complex feelings that may arise – shame, fear, disappointment. Acknowledge the discomfort, instead of trying to bat it away or bury it.

Take another step closer and imagine your Shadow doing the same.

As you close the space between you, notice your Shadow's shape begin to shift. With each step closer, imagine your Shadow taking on a quality that belongs to you, until finally, you find yourself facing . . . yourself.

Look into your Shadow's eyes – your eyes – and allow yourself a short moment to feel everything that has passed between you. Take a deep breath, and on the exhale, nod to your Shadow – to yourself, in a moment of recognition for what you've endured, at each other's hands, and together.

If it feels right, tell your Shadow that you understand. Hear it echo your words.

Share one last look before you let this visualization fall away. Bring yourself back into the room you're in and allow your eyes to open.

Now, reach for your journal, and reflect on your experience.

- How did it feel to look directly at your Shadow?
- How did it feel to allow your Shadow to look directly at you?
- Did anything about your experience surprise you?
- What did this experience help you to understand about your Shadow?
- How can you care for yourself as you recover from this intense experience?

Shadow support

Confronting your Shadow can sometimes result in feeling untethered from your daily life. It's important to make sure that you're tending to yourself and your needs so you can stay grounded even whilst working through big things with your Shadow. As always, consider taking a moment to practise one or more of the Week Three Shadow Self-Care tips on p. 81.

When you feel ready, return to this book for the next step on your Shadow Path.

EXERCISE FOUR: SHADOW SELFIE

For this creative exercise, you'll practise getting comfortable identifying with – and embodying – your Shadow by taking, or creating, self-portraits that highlight your Shadow side.

By confronting your Shadow, you've taken crucial steps to integrate it. You've recognized your Shadow as something not separate or foreign to you, but inherent to you, valuable to the make-up of who you are.

But that growing awareness won't stick if you're not actively taking strides to welcome your Shadow as a critical ingredient of your identity.

In the last exercise, you explored the idea of seeing your Shadow as a reflection of you, as you already are. You imagined that the closer you get to understanding your Shadow, the more of yourself you find there. You realized that confronting your Shadow and confronting yourself are two sides of the same coin.

Now, you can take that growing sense of the connection between you and your Shadow a step further by creating a Shadow-inspired self-portrait.

In doing so, you'll join a long tradition of artists who explored their own depths by depicting themselves in their art. The works of Frida Kahlo, Pablo Picasso and Vincent Van Gogh captured their physical likenesses while also infusing mood and meaning into their work that extended beyond the mirror images of their faces. Vivian Maier used literal shadows as motifs in her self-portraiture, photographers David Uzochukwu and Jo Smith intentionally play with taboo in their work, simultaneously capturing the face they show to the world and challenging the viewer with uncomfortable imagery.

You will need
- A quiet, peaceful place where you can sit or lie down
- A timer
- At least 45 minutes of your time
- A camera, and/or art supplies such as coloured pencils, pens, paints, clay, collage materials
- Your journal and something to write with
- Optional: Costumes, make-up and props

Create a self-portrait of your Shadow

Start in your journal by brainstorming ideas. Think about what a self-portrait that simultaneously captures you and your Shadow – or that represents you on your Shadow journey so far – might look like. You can jot down notes, start to sketch out your ideas or even use collage materials to make a mood board. Think about what medium you might like to use – photography, charcoal, watercolour, collage, clay, mixed media?

Consider what props and materials you'll need. Do you want to include certain objects that represent your Shadow, or design a costume or make-up that helps you express your vision?

Then, gather your materials and props, and get to work making your Shadow self-portrait. Don't be afraid to experiment and feel encouraged to check in with yourself throughout.

As you create ask yourself:

- ▶ What feels most authentic to what I know about the bond my Shadow and I are building?
- ▶ How can I simply but effectively capture how I see my Shadow, how I see myself and the depths I haven't yet discovered?
- ▶ What is being revealed to me about my Shadow through this creative process?

When your work is complete, put it somewhere private and safe, but commit to taking it out for viewing on a regular basis (maybe each time you return to this book to journey further down your Shadow Path).

Shadow and all

Remember, this exercise is about revealing the ways in which your Shadow is an inherent part of you, so don't fall into the trap of trying to create some perfect, idealized version of you. Pop artist Andy Warhol once admitted to removing his pimples and scars from his self-portraits, but you're encouraged to capture yourself honestly, exactly as you are, warts – literal and metaphorical – and all.

If you feel like the work you created perpetuates the neglect and rejection you've perpetrated against your Shadow, don't beat yourself up. Undoing the urge to hide away the parts of yourself you're learning to uncover along your Shadow Path doesn't happen overnight. Instead of taking on guilt, review your journalling notes after the See your Shadow visualization (see p. 91), and invite yourself to create a new iteration of your Shadow self-portrait that more effectively captures the qualities you share with your Shadow.

As always, consider taking a moment to practise one or more of the Week Three Shadow Self-Care tips on p. 81.

When you feel ready, return to this book for the next step on your Shadow Path.

Week Three Reflection Prompts

This week you've upped the ante and faced some of the most challenging terrain on your Shadow Path: you've confronted your Shadow – and yourself – by acknowledging the hurt you've caused each other and accepting the important, unbreakable connection between you.

Now, as your third week on the Shadow Path comes to a close, set your timer for 15 minutes and reflect back on the week in your journal.

Ask yourself
- What did I discover about my Shadow this week?
- Which exercise from this week taught me the most?
- Which exercise from this week was the most joyful?
- What support and comfort could I benefit from before heading into the next week?

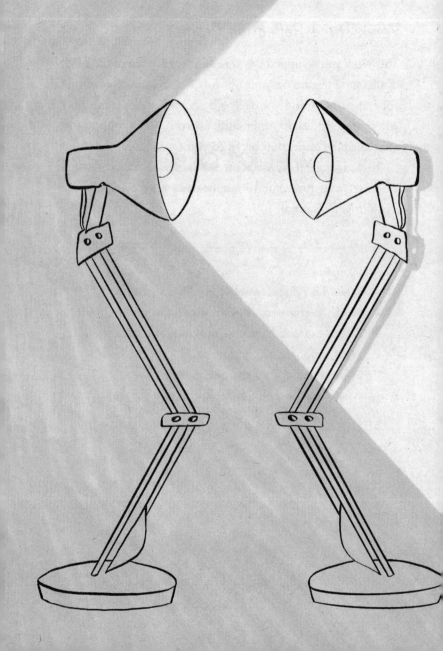

WEEK FOUR:
ILLUMINATE YOUR SHADOW

This week, you'll balance out the challenging elements of your Shadow by seeking out the many gifts tucked away within it, and bringing them into the light.

Through Week Three's exercises, you challenged yourself to confront your Shadow. You faced some of the darkest parts of yourself head-on, and acknowledged, perhaps for the very first time, some of the pain you've experienced and the pain you've caused by burying your fears, desires and shames beneath the surface.

While the road to healing is a long one, the work doesn't have to be relentless. This week is all about coming up for air – and bringing some of the most beautiful treasures in your depths back up to the surface.

The truth is, for every painful mess your Shadow harbours, a gift lies in wait, too.

You know by now that it's not just the negatives that we bury. Beautiful things can find their way to the depths of our unconscious, too. Curiosity, body confidence, creativity, silliness, passion, innocence . . . qualities like these can be buried just as easily as anger, resentment and envy.

You might have buried beautiful things about you for any number of reasons. Maybe someone in your life told you the beautiful things about you weren't valuable. Maybe you were taught that certain qualities or interests you expressed were trivial. Maybe you felt that you had to put aside your most authentic self to make room for socially acceptable ways of being. Maybe you didn't feel safe, so you felt the need to put the beautiful things somewhere where no one – not even you – could get to them.

Whatever the reason, there's no denying that a reconnection with the beautiful treasures you've buried within yourself is long overdue.

But while Week Four is about balancing out the pain you confronted in Week Three, don't expect it to be a complete walk in the park – the Shadow Path is not for the faint of heart, even when the light peeks through the trees.

Prepare yourself for some discomfort as you adjust to the light. Because here's the thing: teasing out the light comes less naturally than hunting down the darkness. It can be uncomfortable, and confronting in its own way, to reckon with the babies you tossed out along with the bathwater. Being willing to take a fresh look at parts of yourself you hid away and see them for the treasure they are may feel difficult, confusing or impossible at first.

Your job this week is to trust the process. To be open to what you might find glittering in your depths when you're brave enough to strike a match and peer into the darkness. To prioritize discovery and allow your curiosity to trump your discomfort.

SHADOW SELF-CARE FOR WEEK FOUR

This week is all about finding the treasures buried in your Shadow, but it's important to remain thoughtful and engaged in your self-care practices, even when dipping into the lighter side of your Shadow Path. If you've got the chance to catch your breath while walking gentler terrain, why not ensure those breaths are deep, cleansing and grounding so that you're properly prepared for what's to come?

Week Four self-care prompts

▶ Schedule a time this week to watch the sun set and/ or rise. Take joy in observing the interplay of light and dark and find the beauty in both.

▶ Seek out the beauty in small things this week, and record what you notice through notes, or by snapping pictures on your phone.

▶ Give gifts this week – to yourself, and to the people in your life. Gifts can be material, but they don't have to be: words of affirmation, consenting physical affection, quality time and acts of service are also beautiful offerings to make.

EXERCISE ONE: SHADOW BY CANDLELIGHT

In this meditative exercise, you'll practise a ritual for connecting with your Shadow by observing the physical dance between light and shadow that occurs when a candle is lit.

Shadow is a product of light. The two are inextricable: where light shines, a shadow is cast. They're two sides of the same coin, and the more open we become to the interplay between them, to the way each illuminates the treasure of the other, the more we can understand the things that highlight, and the things that obscure, the truth of who we are.

In this sensory experience, you're invited to pay attention to the endless interplay of darkness and illumination as a means of exploring your own metaphorical light and shadow.

To get the most out of this exercise, aim to leave analysis at the door and focus instead on the sensory experience.

Some practical tips

This meditation works best with a birthday candle, since it will likely burn out on its own in the time needed for the exercise, but you can swap it out for a tealight or other candle and a timer set for 15 minutes if needed.

Support your birthday candle to stand upright using clay, a paper clip or even a cake that you can treat yourself to when the exercise comes to an end.

Practise safe candle use – never leave a flame unattended, keep it out of the vicinity of any flammable items, pets or children, and know how to reach your fire department in case of emergency. If you have any reservations about using a candle, you can do a flame-free version of this exercise by pulling up a video of a burning candle or fireplace instead.

Read over the guide below a few times before diving in, since you won't be able to reference the text in the dark.

You will need
- A dark, quiet room
- A birthday candle and a match
- 20 minutes of your time
- Your journal and something to write with

Connect with your Shadow by candlelight

Prepare your space: place your candle on a solid, sturdy surface and position a chair or cushion on the floor, in a place where you'll be able to see the candle up close while seated.

Light your candle, set your timer if needed, turn off the lights and sit down.

Train your eyes on the candle flame, taking time to watch it flicker and dance, tugging against the wick. Let the light source become the only focus of your vision.

After a moment, expand your gaze, noticing what the light touches. Take note of what catches your attention, of how ordinary things look different when illuminated by candlelight.

Notice too, what the light doesn't touch – what pockets of darkness appear in your vision, and how you see those spaces differently, too.

Take in the movement, the way light and shadow shift and dance as the flame moves.

Take a deep inhale and breathe out, slow and controlled, in the direction of the flame. Notice how it changes with the motion of your breath.

Sit in this space, soaking up the way that shadow and light melt together, merging and separating as the flame burns on, paying attention in turn to the illuminated details of your space, and the parts shrouded in shadow.

When the candle burns out, or your timer goes off, close your eyes and take a deep breath, letting the imprint of the flame linger on the back of your eyelids. Notice the contrast between dark and light in your mind's eye. Breathe in, and open your eyes on the next exhale.

Turn on the lights and put out your candle if it's still burning. Watch the smoke dissipate and the wax cool and harden.

Reach for your journal and pen and reflect on your experience:

▶ What was this experience like? What did you notice? How did you feel?
▶ How did meditating on the candle, and what its flame did and didn't illuminate, reflect your growing understanding of your Shadow?
▶ Did anything about your experience surprise you?
▶ What did this experience help you to understand about your Shadow?

Sacred Shadow

Candles have a special place in spiritual work – Catholics light them for saints, the Hindu festival of Diwali uses candles to symbolize wishes for the new year, Taoists display candles on their altars to represent the duality of light and dark, and practitioners of witchcraft and folk magic use candles to focus their energy when casting spells and performing rituals.

If you found this exercise compelling, consider incorporating candles into your Shadow Work sessions more often, as a means of making the time sacred and special. You could burn a special candle that represents your Shadow or continue to use birthday candles to avoid the buzz of a timer. Again, just be sure to practise fire safety: never leave a candle burning unattended, and steer clear of lighting candles near any flammable objects like cloth or paper.

As always, consider taking a moment to practise one or more of the Week Four Shadow Self-Care tips on p. 104.

When you feel ready, return to this book for the next step on your Shadow Path.

EXERCISE TWO: SHADOW TREASURE

In this journalling exercise, you'll dig deep to excavate the hidden beauty hiding in your Shadow. You'll unbury lost talents, pleasures and desires so that you return them to the surface and enjoy them in your life.

Writer Joseph Campbell, who popularized the Hero's Journey narrative theory once said that 'Where you stumble, there lies your treasure. The very cave you are afraid to enter turns out to be the source of what you are looking for.'[4]

Campbell, whose perspective on storytelling was informed by archetypal patterns braided through ancient myths all the way up to trends in modern psychological frameworks, wasn't only fascinated by the archetypal Hero. His work, because of its interest in the conflict between good and evil, explores the flipside of heroism, too: a concept that, like the Shadow, is not at all what it seems.

The Hero's Journey – which we'll explore in depth later along your Shadow Path in Week Nine (see p. 225) – has also been described as an allegorical quest that charts a path from what's known, through what's unknown, to deeper understanding and wisdom, and back again. It's easy to see how this story mirrors what you do, every time you set foot on your Shadow Path. You leave the known world, journey into the abyss and resurface with new knowledge about yourself.

In writing about the cave of treasures that lies where we

stumble, Campbell recognized that the most powerful stories find value in the dark. The drama and catharsis that heroic myths – ancient and modern – bring forth are most effective when the Hero is not only willing to look within themself and confront their demons, but to find hidden treasure (or, to borrow a term Campbell used often, 'elixir') there in the process; elixir worth bringing back to the surface, for all the benefits it has to offer the Hero, and their wider community.

Last week in Week Three, you did the heroic work of stepping into a cave you were afraid to enter to confront your Shadow. Your quest today is to identify the treasures there: the pleasures you denied yourself, the qualities you learned to mask, the dreams you put aside and the memories that were beautiful, yet painful, to summon.

You will need
- A quiet, peaceful place where you can write
- A timer
- 20 minutes of your time
- Your journal and something to write with

Find and examine your treasure

Set your timer for 20 minutes and turn to your journal and your pen.

Explore the following questions until the timer goes off:

- What treasures are hidden in my Shadow?
- Why might I have stashed that treasure there?
- How might bringing this treasure back out into the light make my life better?
- How might bringing this treasure back out into the light make life better for my community?
- Why am I afraid to accept these treasures as gifts?
- What's one element of my Shadow treasure that I can bring back to the surface with me today?

Shadow gold

This exercise is one you can return to often – the treasure within your Shadow is a living thing, evolving and growing and appreciating as you invest in your Shadow Path.

Think of these prompts as the equivalent of panning for gold in your own psyche. Sometimes you'll find nothing but faint glitter, other times you'll dredge up nuggets as big as your fist. It's always worth checking to see what you can find.

And, as you continue to mine your Shadow for the treasure it holds, remember to thank it for keeping these parts of you safe.

As always, consider taking a moment to practise one or more of the Week Four Shadow Self-Care tips on p. 104.

When you feel ready, return to this book for the next step on your Shadow Path.

EXERCISE THREE: SHADOW TROPHIES

In this creative exercise, you'll reflect on everything you've discovered that your Shadow has to offer and reward it for the positive things it can bring to your life.

The idea of the 'participation trophy' has had an increasingly bad rap in recent years. Pundits have lambasted the practice, which rose to prominence between the late 80s and early 2000s, as coddling.

And yet, the philosophy behind the participation trophy is sound: the participation prize was always meant to engender resilience, to teach children that success is a journey. Rewarding participation recognizes that showing up is valuable in its own right.

That message provides the safety and security needed to keep pushing. It teaches young people that they are valuable whether they win or lose, whether they are 'good' or 'bad'. Armed with that foundation of confidence, anyone would feel more comfortable continuing to show up. And when you keep showing up, you learn. You improve. You evolve. You discover a version of success that feels safe, secure and rewarding for you. A version of success that doesn't try to erase failure, but rather accepts it as a recurring landmark on the journey to a more fulfilled life.

The participation trophy shines a light on the value of showing up, and it's wise to adopt a similar approach to working with your Shadow. Reward the hidden parts of you that find their way to the surface for showing up. That's enough. And reward yourself for being open to witnessing them. That's enough, too.

In that spirit, today you're going to make, and present, some Shadow trophies.

> You will need
> - A quiet, peaceful place
> - A timer
> - 45 minutes of your time
> - Art supplies, such as paper and coloured pencils, collage materials and/or design software
> - Your journal and something to write with

Make a Shadow trophy

Set a timer for 5 minutes and list all the things you appreciate about your Shadow in your journal.

Once you have your list, gaze back over it and choose an item on the list that really represents what makes your Shadow inherently valuable.

From there, you're going to craft a trophy that represents this valuable quality, using any artistic or craft medium of your choice.

Don't put any pressure on yourself to make it 'good' by an external critic's standards. (This is sound advice for every creative exercise in this book, but is particularly relevant to today's.)

Once you've crafted your trophy, imagine presenting it to your Shadow. You can speak out loud about the reasons it's earned this reward, or write them down in your journal.

Display your trophy somewhere you'll see it often.

Play Shadow games, win Shadow prizes

A crucial component of illuminating – and ultimately, integrating – your Shadow is getting comfortable acknowledging what it naturally brings to the table. When you reward your Shadow for being valuable exactly as it already is, when you validate the unique magic it has to offer your life, the treasures that your Shadow is willing to share with you are going to multiply.

In other words, when you show up for your Shadow, you teach it to show up for you.

Throughout the rest of this week, allow yourself to reflect on and appreciate the simple victory that you and your Shadow share every day you choose to acknowledge each other. Make note of the rewards you're beginning to reap as a result of your participation in Shadow Work and Play.

As always, consider taking a moment to practise one or more of the Week Four Shadow Self-Care tips on p. 104.

When you feel ready, return to this book for the next step on your Shadow Path.

EXERCISE FOUR: DIVINE YOUR SHADOW

For this exercise, you'll learn how to use tools like tarot cards, pendulums, and books of poetry to connect with your Shadow and shine a light on what it wants to tell you.

Sometimes you may need a little help shining a light on your Shadow and discovering what gifts lie in wait for you. Divination practices can come in handy when you're struggling to see into your depths clearly: they can function like a compass, guiding you where you need to go and helping you to see things you may have missed.

The word 'divination' itself suggests a communion with the divine – a process of revelation and a journey to deeper wisdom. And while some spiritual modalities concentrate on the power of tools like tarot cards to predict what might happen in the future, fortune-telling is just one flavour in a larger suite of assets that divination tools have to offer. Divination can play a role in many spiritual and self-discovery practices, from channelling spirits to journalling and creative inspiration to psychoanalytic explorations.

Like Shadow exploration, divination methods sit at a powerful intersection of the spiritual and psychological. Take it from Carl Jung, the father of modern Shadow Work and a devotee of the Chinese divination method, the *I Ching*, or the *Book of Changes*. In a 1949 foreword to a new translation of the *I Ching*, Jung wrote: 'The method of the I Ching does indeed take into account the hidden individual quality in things and men, and in one's own unconscious self as well.'⁵

Today, give yourself permission to play with and explore how you might cultivate a personal divination practice that helps you take into account what's hidden within you, by shining a light on what your Shadow is ready to reveal to you in this moment.

> You will need
> - A quiet, peaceful place
> - About 20 minutes of your time
> - Tarot or oracle cards, a book of poems and/or a pendulum
> - Your journal and something to write with
> - if using a pendulum, a piece of paper on which to write YES and NO

Experiment with divination

Here are three ways you can experiment with using divination tools to shine a light on your Shadow:

1. Use a **tarot or oracle deck** to ask your Shadow open-ended questions. All you need to do is shuffle the deck of cards you've chosen to work with, take a deep breath, ask your

question, draw a single card and reflect on all of the possible answers the card you've drawn might represent.

Some of my favourite questions are:

▶ What gift would you like to give me?
▶ How can I be more compassionate to you?
▶ What do you need me to know?
▶ What needs to come to the surface?
▶ How can we work together towards fulfilment?

Record your reflections in your journal, and then ask yourself:

▶ What story is your Shadow telling you through the card?
▶ How can understanding this story help you and your Shadow understand each other better?
▶ What do you want to reflect on further/ask your Shadow more about?

If you like this method, you can experiment with drawing a card every day to represent a message from your Shadow.

2. If you're intrigued by the idea of using divination to explore open-ended questions with your Shadow but don't have a tarot or oracle deck to hand, you can try **bibliomancy** instead. This is one of the simplest, most accessible forms of divination and it requires only a book! I personally recommend

using a book of poems, as they tend to offer the deepest, most thought-provoking answers, but you can use any book that calls to you. Dictionaries can be a lot of fun, and very forthcoming.

Come to your book prepared with a few open questions you'd like to ask your Shadow – you can try the same prompts offered in the preceding tarot section.

Choose a question to work with. Then close your eyes, take a deep breath, focus on the question you wish to ask your Shadow and flip through the pages as you exhale. When you're ready to inhale again, open your eyes and read the page you've landed on. Take note of lines that stand out to you and write them down in your journal. Reflect on how they answer, and bring a new perspective to, the question you asked.

3. Use a **pendulum** to ask your Shadow yes or no questions. You can buy a pendulum at most spiritual stockists, but you can also make your own by threading a heavy ring onto a cord. Write YES on the right hand side of a piece of paper and NO on the left hand side.

To use your pendulum, hold the top of the cord between the pads of your index finger and thumb, with the ring or weight hanging down over the centre of your piece of paper. Keep your hand as still as possible and start by gently asking your pendulum a series of yes/no questions you know the answer to, such as 'Is A the first letter of the alphabet?' or 'Is the sky green?' Take note of how the pendulum moves on a no and how it moves on a yes, and continue asking obvious questions until you feel tuned into its behaviour. You are then ready to ask your Shadow some yes or no questions such as:

- Do you feel connected to me?
- Are you afraid of me?
- Do you feel seen and respected by me?

Stick to a maximum of five or six questions, and avoid antagonizing or advice-led questions like 'Do you hate me?' or 'Should I do X?' – remember that in this context divination is a tool for reflection and connection.

When you've finished your session, record your Shadow's responses in your journal, and reflect on your own emotional reactions to the answers you received. What do these answers reveal about your Shadow? What do they prompt you to do? How can this knowledge enrich your relationship with your Shadow?

Speak your Shadow's language

When practising the art of divination, especially as it pertains to your Shadow Path journey, it's important to make sure that you take lots of time to reflect on the information you receive from your Shadow to ensure that you aren't acting impulsively or based on unformed assumptions.

Think of these tools as aids in helping you and your Shadow get on the same page, speak the same language. Divination is all about fuelling discovery and exploring options – it's not a direct order, from some external spiritual being or even from your own depths. It's simply a different way of connecting, one that can help you open new doors and discover new avenues for exploration and discovery along your Shadow path.

As always, consider taking a moment to practise one or more of the Week Four Shadow Self-Care tips on p. 104.

When you feel ready, return to this book for the next step on your Shadow Path.

Week Four Reflection Prompts

This week, you've worked towards a more evolved – and dazzling – perspective of your Shadow Path. You've looked into the dark and illuminated the beautiful things hiding in your Shadow by reflecting on the relationship between shadow and light, seeking out the treasures hidden in your unconscious; you've rewarded parts of yourself you used to hide away and learned new tactics to shine a light on your Shadow's point of view.

Now, as your fourth week on the Shadow Path comes to a close, set your timer for 15 minutes and reflect back on the week in your journal.

Ask yourself
- What did I discover about my Shadow this week?
- Which exercise from this week taught me the most?
- Which exercise from this week was the most joyful?
- What support and comfort could I benefit from before heading into the next week?

WEEK FIVE:
EMBRACE YOUR SHADOW

This week, you'll take everything that you've been through with your Shadow so far and find the confidence to own and accept your Shadow self as an integral part of who you are at your core.

The ultimate aim of Shadow Work is a radical acceptance of everything that makes you who you are – the light, the dark, the knowns, the unknowns, your conscious and unconscious self.

Carl Jung called the progress towards this acceptance 'integration', an ability to sit simultaneously in light and shadow . . . to not only own both of these parts of yourself, but to recognize them as inextricable from each other. In 1959, Jung wrote:

> *To confront a person with his shadow is to show him his own light. Once one has experienced a few times what it is like to stand judgingly between the opposites, one begins to understand what is meant by the self. Anyone who perceives his shadow and his light simultaneously sees himself from two sides and thus gets in the middle.*[6]

Why cast out, shame or judge your Shadow aspects when you can meet yourself, for all that you truly are, right in the middle? Why not perceive your Shadow in tandem with the light, and come to know yourself more fully?

This powerful meeting in the middle isn't a concept unique to Jungian psychology: spiritual seekers have been on a quest to understand and honour the equally critical roles that shadow and light play in the human experience for centuries. Taoists use the yin yang as a visual symbol for the balance of light and dark that is intrinsic to consciousness. In many pagan traditions, solstices and equinoxes hold special power, due to the symbolic significance of night meeting day, dark meeting light.

Even Christianity, which in its modern iterations tends to demonize the darkness within us as sin, honours both light and dark within its creation myth: God doesn't banish darkness forever when he creates light, he divides the natural rhythm of life into two halves: night and day.

In storytelling, a hero can't save the day unless they have first descended to their depths and endured a 'dark night of the soul' . . . their wins lack meaning unless they first understand the pain of loss.

All this is to say that your Shadow – with its sharp edges and its soft underbelly – is part of you. It is a spiritual and psychological organ that plays a critical role in your story. Coming to accept and embrace your Shadow is the act of coming to accept and embrace yourself.

This week, you reach the halfway point of your journey through this book. So far, you've wandered down this path on your own, mostly observing your Shadow from a distance, contemplating and exploring it without fully stepping into those depths.

But now, as you find yourself at this midway point, it's time to join forces with your Shadow . . . to submerge yourself in your own depths and take in all that you are. It's time to reach out your hand and grasp your Shadow, so that you can complete the rest of this journey as companions on the Shadow Path.

It's time to meet in the middle, where Shadow and light dance together as equals, and forge a new partnership that eclipses the way you conceived of your Shadow, and yourself, before.

SHADOW SELF-CARE FOR WEEK FIVE

This week, you'll tie together everything you've experienced on your Shadow Path so far and take strides to welcome the Shadow you've come to know into your life. This can be a transformational experience, but it's also important to keep yourself grounded and leave space and time for yourself so that you can rest and recover. As always, practising intentional self-care and self-regulation strategies will be critical while you navigate this challenging stretch of your Shadow Path.

You can turn to any of the self-care tips you've learned from this book so far, rely on your own personal preferred self-care strategies or try any of these:

Week Five self-care prompts

▶ Spend time outdoors and pay attention to the sensations you experience when you commune with nature: the feeling of wind on your skin, of your feet on the earth, the smell of flowers, the chatter of birds and even the noises made by other people.

▶ Journal about experiences outside of your Shadow exploration. Reflect on things that bring you comfort, joy or peace.

▶ Seek out physical comfort: hug the people or

animals in your life or treat yourself to physically
soothing activities like a having a bath or massage or
doing a stretching routine.

EXERCISE ONE: PARDON YOUR SHADOW

In this journalling exercise, you'll revisit the wounds you and your Shadow have caused each other and use the perspective you gained in Week Four to show your Shadow – and yourself – grace, so that you can move forward meaningfully together.

To embrace your Shadow, you must first make peace with the past you've shared.

While that doesn't mean excusing or erasing the harm that has passed between you and your Shadow, it does mean leading with compassion, understanding and good faith. It means choosing forgiveness – of your Shadow and yourself.

But forgiveness is a sensitive subject, and a tricky one when you're in the early stages of navigating your Shadow Path. It can be hard to know how to move forward and release the past without burying it once again.

Over the last month, all the strides you've taken on your Shadow Path have been leading you here: to this fulcrum moment. To the decision to put the past behind you, without ever forgetting where you and your Shadow have come from.

Let's start by looking to the very recent past: just two weeks ago in Week Three, when you first began to confront your Shadow, you drafted a pair of Victim Impact Statements (see p. 87). The first addressed your Shadow, calling it out for the way it has caused you harm. The second challenged you, from your Shadow's point of view, by identifying the ways that your neglect and rejection of your full self have hurt your Shadow.

At the time, you were encouraged to sit with what you'd written, without feeling rushed to offer forgiveness or make amends.

Since then, through Week Four's mission to illuminate your Shadow, you've done important work to recognize the beauty in your depths and allow yourself to see a vision for the future in which you and your Shadow trade past wounds for mutual appreciation.

Armed with that new perspective, it's time now to offer your Shadow, and yourself, forgiveness so that you can move forward.

You will need
- A quiet, peaceful place
- About 30 minutes of your time
- Your notes from the Victim Impact Statement exercise from Week Three
- Your journal and something to write with

Pardon your Shadow

Get out your journal and set your timer for 20–30 minutes.

Using your Victim Impact Statements for reference, write

a letter of pardon for your Shadow, granting it clemency for its past crimes, and acknowledging your own.

You don't have to forgive everything just now if it doesn't feel right but make an effort in the letter to acknowledge what you *are* ready to offer grace for, even if it feels challenging.

Shadow grace

The Jungian psychoanalyst and spiritual writer Clarissa Pinkola Estes, once called forgiveness 'an act of creation'. She proposed that forgiveness is not some one-and-done bridge to be crossed and forgotten, but instead an ongoing, intentional choice. Something we do to make space for other things: love, acceptance, peace, wisdom.[7]

As you move forward with a new sense of perspective and peace about your past experiences with your Shadow, be prepared to return to this letter of pardon as a reminder that you choose grace, even if future moments arise where showing grace to your Shadow and yourself feels difficult.

As always, consider taking a moment to practise one or more of the Week Five Shadow Self-Care tips on p. 129.

When you feel ready, return to this book for the next step on your Shadow Path.

EXERCISE TWO: MAKE YOUR SHADOW FEEL AT HOME

For this visualization exercise, you'll step into a new level of intimacy with your Shadow by imagining a scenario where you invite it over and welcome it into your home.

Start by reading through the following visualization journey before closing your eyes and trying it for yourself. You don't need to memorize the entire journey; simply read through to get a sense of the content, and then lead yourself through the major points, staying open to where your own mind and soul lead you.

If you're more comfortable following the script exactly, you can journal your way through this exercise instead of doing it with eyes closed.

You will need
- A private, quiet space
- A timer
- 25 minutes of your time
- Your journal and something to write with

Visualization to welcome your Shadow into your home

When you're ready to start, set the timer for 15 minutes.

Begin by closing your eyes and taking several deep breaths.

As you continue to breathe, imagine yourself at home, preparing for the arrival of a visitor. In your mind's eye, walk yourself through the things you might do to prime your space for a guest – perhaps boiling water for coffee, tidying the room where you will receive them or lighting a candle.

Take care in visualizing each small action. Consider what you might hear, feel, see or smell as you ready your home for a visitor.

After a moment, imagine a knock at your front door. Pay attention to the quality of the knock – is it soft or loud, hesitant or confident, short or long? What does this tell you about the energy of your visitor?

Imagine yourself approaching the door, placing your hand on the knob and swinging it open to reveal your Shadow on the other side.

Take several deep breaths as the two of you stand at the threshold. Give yourself this moment to take your Shadow in and allow it to do the same.

When you're ready, invite your Shadow into your home.

Notice how it enters, and how you feel as it does. Consider what action you can take to make you, and your Shadow, more comfortable.

Lead your Shadow to the space you've prepared and invite it to sit down. If you've prepared drinks or snacks, offer them and pay attention to how your Shadow responds. Notice what it's drawn to, how it takes its tea or coffee and how it holds itself.

Tell your Shadow gently, kindly, how it feels to have it present in this space with you. Imagine how it might respond, and what it might share with you.

Breathe in the energy between you and sit with it for as long as you feel comfortable.

When the timer goes off – or when the timing feels right – thank your Shadow for coming. Walk it to the door and, if it feels true, tell your Shadow that it's always welcome. If you're not quite ready to extend that full invitation, tell it that you'll call on it soon.

Watch your Shadow retreat, and when you're ready, imagine yourself closing the door. Breathe in the energy you're left with after the encounter, and as you breathe out, let the visualization fall away.

Bring yourself back to the room where you are and open your eyes when it feels right for you to do so.

Reflect on your experience in your journal

▶ How did it feel to welcome your Shadow into your home?

- Was there anything that made you uncomfortable, and why?
- Would you be comfortable inviting your Shadow back into your personal space?
- If you are ready to welcome your Shadow back into your home, how might you receive it next time? What could you discuss or do together?
- If you're not ready to receive your Shadow at home again, what can you do to help yourself get to this point? Would it help to revisit any of the exercises from this book so far?

Air out your Shadow

When you've finished this exercise, consider clearing the energy in your space. This is not because your Shadow carries negative energy, but because the intensity of your encounter at this stage may disrupt you as you move about the responsibilities of your daily life, and clearing your environment can help enforce positive boundaries around your Shadow Work.

You can clear the energy in your home by opening windows, lighting a fresh candle or simmering citrus fruit in water on your stove and allowing the steam to waft through the house. You could also take a bath or shower with your favourite scented products.

If you're making use of candles or stovetops, be careful not to leave any source of fire or heat unattended.

As always, consider taking a moment to practise one or more of the Week Five Shadow Self-Care tips on p. 129.

When you feel ready, return to this book for the next step on your Shadow Path.

EXERCISE THREE: SHADOW CUDDLE

In this somatic exercise, you'll literally embrace your Shadow to build up a sense of physical safety and comfort between you.

The Dutch psychiatrist and author Bessel A. van der Kolk's ground-breaking book *The Body Keeps the Score* argues that psychological and spiritual healing is as much a somatic experience as it is a cerebral one. He writes that 'to change, people need to become aware of their sensations and the way that their bodies interact with the world around them. Physical self-awareness is the first step in releasing the tyranny of the past.'[8]

Van der Kolk preaches that through sensory-based mindfulness, we can learn to rewrite the narratives we live out in our daily lives, and experience a healthier, more compassionate relationship with ourselves – and with all the light and dark parts that form us.

Van der Kolk's work is focused specifically on healing trauma wounds – and while we know that much more than traumatic experiences live within the Shadow, the advice he offers can be hugely useful on your journey to knowing and embracing your Shadow. Physical awareness isn't just the first step in releasing the tyranny of the past, it's a vital ingredient to holding space in the present for all the things we've hidden away.

So much of our Shadow Work and Play takes place in our minds and spirit that it can be easy to forget the body. But, when you do make an effort to engage the body in the process, you won't just make progress on your path towards deeper self-understanding and compassion, you'll chart new pathways by programming love, kindness and acceptance into your muscle memory.

Engaging the body along your Shadow Path can be simple. This exercise doesn't involve any complicated yoga moves or breathing techniques. All you have to do to engage your body on this week's quest to 'Embrace your Shadow' is to, quite literally, embrace your Shadow.

You will need
- A quiet, peaceful place
- About 10 minutes of your time
- A pillow in a case
- Your Shadow Talisman
- Your journal and something to write with

Embrace your Shadow

Take the Shadow Talisman you chose in Week One (see p. 40), slip it into your pillow case and wrap your arms around the pillow. By placing your talisman inside, you cast the smallest spell: imbuing your pillow with the essence of your Shadow so that you can hug it. Now, hug the pillow.

Allow yourself to feel the depth of the intimacy that physically embracing your Shadow creates. Breathe deeply into the sensation of offering this act of care to your Shadow and take note of how the action provides comfort to you, too.

You might try petting, stroking or patting the pillow and speaking affirmations to your Shadow, such as:

'I accept you as you are.'

'You and I are in this together.'

Or 'Everything that you are and everything that I am is welcome here.'

When you feel ready, give your Shadow a final squeeze and release it. Pick up your journal and jot down a few notes on the experience. Ask yourself:

▶ How does it feel to interact physically with my Shadow?
▶ What sensations did I experience in my body during this exercise?
▶ What felt good, and what felt bad?
▶ Did anything shift or change for me as I embraced my Shadow?

Shadow spooning

If it feels right for you, carry on with this practice regularly. Keep your Shadow Talisman in your pillow and spoon it at night, forming a new bond of comfort and care.

You could even try ways of interacting with this huggable stand-in for your Shadow: dance with it (try using the playlist you created in Week One; see p. 44); watch TV or read with the pillow-turned-Shadow propping you up; sit with it in your lap while you complete exercises in this book.

As always, before you move on with your day, consider taking a moment to practise one or more of the Week Five Shadow Self-Care tips on p. 129.

When you feel ready, return to this book for the next step on your Shadow Path.

EXERCISE FOUR: TOTAL ECLIPSE

In this creative exercise, you'll create a visual aide that helps you accept your Shadow as an essential ingredient of what makes you whole. You'll reflect on how your journey down the Shadow Path so far has helped you to create a new relationship with your Shadow that eclipses whatever came before.

At the beginning of this book, I invited you to imagine yourself as the moon, full all the time, even when the world – and your own consciousness – only experiences a fraction of all that you are.

Now I want to invite you to consider a different celestial metaphor to capture your evolving journey on the Shadow Path: the eclipse.

Eclipses are astronomical events defined by shadows – they happen when the moon, a planet or a satellite passes between the earth and the sun, resulting in a shadow being cast.

Solar eclipses are the most visually dramatic. Scientifically, we're witnessing the moon pass in front of the sun and cast a shadow on the earth. But from our perspective on the ground, we see the sun swallowed by darkness. Solar eclipses can occur in three ways: a partial solar eclipse looks like a round shadow has taken a bite out of the sun; in an annular eclipse, the moon's shadow is smaller than the sun, so a solid ring of sunlight remains shining on the earth throughout the event – imagine a wedding ring in the sky; and finally, a total eclipse sees the moon's shadow block out the sun's light entirely, save for a thin, wispy, ghostlike ring of light around the darkness.

'What you see in an eclipse is entirely different from what you know,' wrote memoirist Annie Dillard in an essay recounting her experience of witnessing a total solar eclipse. Later in the piece, she describes a revelation that occurred to her while watching a shadow swallow the light of the sun: 'In the deeps are the violence and terror of which psychology has warned us. But if you ride these monsters deeper down, if you drop with them further over the world's rim, you find what our sciences cannot locate or name, the substrate, the ocean or matrix or ether which buoys the rest, which gives goodness its power for good, and evil its power for evil.'[9]

In other words, witnessing a literal shadow event led Dillard to contemplate the psychological and spiritual experience of the unconscious – of all the good and evil, beauty and violence, light and shadow within us. She goes on to conclude that only when these things are united are we whole.

Eclipses capture the imagination and speak to us on a deeply unconscious level about the vastness, mystery, power, fear and wonder that define the depths of the human experience.

Like Shadow Work and Play, eclipses compel us to look beyond the veil of the normal, to appreciate the strange, arresting beauty of what happens when darkness and light dance together.

The term 'eclipse' has also become a poetic way of expressing when one way of being takes the place of an old one – a step into something greater than what was before. In the march of time, the future always manages to eclipse the past. A new love can eclipse an old heartbreak. A spiritual epiphany can eclipse the world view you once held. The depths you discover on your Shadow Path can eclipse who you thought you were.

For this exercise, you're going to imagine your own Shadow journey as an eclipse event.

You will need
- A quiet, peaceful place
- About 30 minutes of your time
- Art supplies including paper, scissors, markers, pens or pencils
- Your journal and something to write with

Create eclipse-inspired Shadow art

First, cut your paper into a large circle. Don't worry if it's not perfect.

Now, fill the circle with words, phrases or doodles that represent how you saw yourself before you began the journey down your Shadow Path. Get as creative as you want here – play with pattern, colour, size and shape.

When the circle is full, you may wish to snap a photo of what you've made so far.

Next, totally eclipse what you've created by drawing and writing over the top. This time, fill the circle in with words, phrases or doodles that represent everything you've learned about yourself and your Shadow along this journey. As well as including new reflections, you can reference things you've written in your journal and the lyrics of songs on your Shadow playlist. Write and doodle until you've completely covered what you did before.

When you're done, spend a few minutes taking in the art that you've made. A picture of all that you are. Reflect on the change represented here: when you began this journey, your Shadow was hidden beneath your surface. Now, it's staring you in the face, entirely different from what you knew, with all its strange beauty exposed.

Put your eclipse art somewhere safe – you're going to need it at a later point in your journey.

Transformed by Shadow

This unique work of art doesn't just represent one step on your Shadow journey, it represents total transformation.

But of course, the thing about eclipses is they don't last – eventually, the shadow will pass and the normal light of day will return. But the memory, the impact, the change – that lasts.

Embracing your Shadow doesn't mean that you can never

live a normal life, or that your Shadow becomes some kind of ruler over your behaviour. Instead, it's about knowing, and appreciating, the strange, rare beauty your Shadow offers, and welcoming those moments when it does surface.

As always, before you move on with your day, consider taking a moment to practise one or more of the Week Five Shadow Self-Care tips on p. 129.

When you feel ready, return to this book for the next step on your Shadow Path.

Week Five Reflection Prompts

This week you've reflected back on everything you've learned about yourself and your Shadow and taken strides to accept and welcome your Shadow as a valued part of who you are. You've forgiven yourself and your Shadow for past hurts, embraced the gifts your Shadow has to offer, and begun to welcome your Shadow into your life.

Now, as your fifth week on the Shadow Path comes to a close, set your timer for 15 minutes and reflect back on the week in your journal.

Ask yourself
- What did I discover about my Shadow this week?
- Which exercise from this week taught me the most?
- Which exercise from this week was the most joyful?
- What support and comfort could I benefit from before heading into the next week?

WEEK SIX:
SOOTHE YOUR SHADOW

This week, you'll confront what spurs you to bury certain experiences, feelings, desires and impulses in your Shadow. You'll work towards developing tools to help you treat your Shadow better.

Robert Louis Stevenson's famous novella, *The Strange Case of Doctor Jekyll and Mr Hyde* centres around a good, upstanding doctor and his murderous, unconscious alter ego. It explores what happens when we refuse to acknowledge anything shameful within us. Jekyll tries to sever himself from his darkest impulses – the things he was hiding (or Hyde-ing, as it were) from the world. The experiment backfires: Jekyll frees his dark side to run rampant all over London, and he's powerless to stop it.

Stevenson's story is often cited in conversations around Shadow as an example of the dangers we face when we lose control of ourselves. Stevenson suggests that our Shadow, after a lifetime of repression, takes its revenge by 'acting out' all the dark and unsavoury impulses we've buried deep inside ourselves.

While it's a striking narrative, and a real page turner, *The Strange Case of Doctor Jekyll and Mr Hyde* doesn't really do your Shadow any justice.

You know by now that your Shadow is no monster, and

it's not the source of your worst impulses – it's simply the secret place where you're used to hiding them. Your Shadow doesn't act out – *you* do, because you don't know how to cope with or acknowledge the parts of you that you feel ashamed or scared of. Hyde was always just Jekyll, and even though he succeeded in burying his guilt and conscious experiences of his wrongdoings, his actions still hurt people, and himself. The Shadow may be vast, but it can't always hold everything – rage, in particular, has a habit of bursting out, and when it does, we settle for burying whatever we can: the sense of guilt and responsibility for the damage we caused.

If only the doctor had had the emotional fortitude to confront the parts of himself that he feared instead of first imprisoning them and then trying to eradicate them, the story might have had a happy ending.

So, if there's one Shadow lesson we can learn from this cautionary tale of a good man gone bad, it's that you have to acknowledge and treat your wounds – do not try to throw them in the trash. If you don't, you risk losing yourself entirely.

Acknowledging this uncomfortable truth is, of course, a critical tenet of Shadow Work and Play: the things we are ashamed of don't deserve our abandonment or neglect, and our Shadows do not deserve to be reduced to a landfill for things we'd rather not face.

If you want to advance on this journey, it's time to move beyond exploring your Shadow, and step into actively building a better relationship with it. This begins by committing to no longer misusing it as convenient storage for all the things you don't want to deal with, and instead taking responsibility and ownership of the way you treat your Shadow, even in your worst moments.

This week, you'll explore what life can look like when you actively choose not to bury uncomfortable or overwhelming emotions, experiences and impulses in your Shadow. You'll get familiar with the warning signs that indicate you might be about to misuse your Shadow; you'll experiment with new coping mechanisms that can help you confront challenging emotions, experiences and impulses in the moment, and you'll commit to working with your Shadow instead of saddling it with the unfair burden of carrying what you don't want to hold.

SHADOW SELF-CARE FOR WEEK SIX

This week is all about practising self-care and self-regulation strategies to help you tame the impulse to bury your challenging emotions, experiences and impulses in your Shadow, so you'll receive plenty of self-care recommendations as you move through each exercise.

With that said, I do have one important self-care tip for you to follow this week:

Week Six self-care prompt

▶ Revisit Week 5, exercise one: 'Pardon your Shadow' (p. 131) before you go any further this week. The work of taking responsibility for the things that prompt you to mistreat your Shadow can be confronting and guilt-inducing, so it's important to remember the grace that you're committed to showing yourself as you walk your Shadow journey. Reread your letter of pardon any time you feel guilt creep back into your soul this week.

If and when you need extra self-care, refer back to previous chapters in this book or notes in your journal and repeat any of the strategies you've already used along your Shadow Path.

EXERCISE ONE: SHADOW TRIGGERS

In this journalling exercise, you're going to explore the experiences, places and people that trigger you to misuse your Shadow.

Imagine this scenario: you watch a video about why people with your complexion shouldn't wear certain colours, and you become self-conscious about having those colours in your wardrobe. Even though you love a particular colour, you stop wearing it – you bury your self-expression and personal preference to avoid the shame and fear you feel about how you and your body are perceived. Eventually, you forget you ever liked the colour at all.

Years later, if you're lucky, you turn back to yourself and start hunting out the things you used to love. There, waiting for you in your Shadow is that beautiful colour. The self-consciousness is still there, but you're learning not to let it define you. And for the first time in a long time, you allow yourself to love what you love more than fearing what you fear.

So far along your Shadow journey, you've focused on rediscovering all the feelings, experiences and impulses you've buried in your Shadow. But now it's time to reflect on what it is that triggers you to bury anything there in the first place.

But first, because the word 'trigger' has become an overused buzzword in conversations around mental health and trauma, let's briefly define what a trigger is in the context of your personal journey to understand, respect and work with your Shadow. For our purposes, a trigger is anything that might prompt you to hide part of your true self away. Usually, a Shadow trigger is a complex mix of what happens to us, and what we do with that experience.

Take the example above: the video casts a judgement about what is acceptable for you, and that sets off your self-consciousness. You don't like being self-conscious. It's uncomfortable. You want to free yourself from the painful experience, and so you try to dispose of it entirely by burying everything that you associate with this particular self-consciousness (in this case, you'd associate the self-consciousness with the colour) in a convenient place where you don't have to think about it – your Shadow.

The triggers here are the stepping stones to misusing your Shadow. You've learned by now that your Shadow is not a receptacle for the parts of your human experience you want to dispose of, but you still need practice to keep yourself from falling back into old habits.

When we experience things we don't like, things that make us feel uncomfortable, it's only natural to want to shove them as far away from our consciousness as possible. But by learning what kinds of emotions and experiences you can't bear (like being judged, being told what to do or feeling self-conscious), you can become more mindful of how you process those emotions instead of just hiding the unprocessed feeling away in your Shadow.

In this exercise, you'll take steps to start identifying and understanding what triggers you to misuse your Shadow, so that you can make more compassionate decisions that honour the truth of who you are and protect your Shadow from bearing the brunt of your painful experiences alone.

You will need
- A peaceful, quiet place
- A timer
- 1 hour of your time
- Your journal and something to write with

Here's what you're going to do:

To start, have your journal to hand and set the timer for 10 minutes.

Make a list of all the things you've discovered hidden in your Shadow so far on this journey, including talents, desires, fears and memories, and anything else you've uncovered as you've walked along your Shadow Path. Try to be specific. Examples may include: 'My dream of singing in a band', 'My natural intuition', 'My suspicion that my parents weren't meeting my emotional needs', 'My anger at the kids who bullied me', 'My sensitivity to other people's emotions' or 'My curiosity about sex'.

If it helps, take some time to review past entries in your Shadow Journal to jog your memory.

Write each thing at the top of a new page in your journal – you're going to be returning to reflect on them in more depth in the next part of the exercise.

When the timer goes off and you have your list ready, review each item on your list. Reflect on each item one by one by answering the following questions beneath each entry in your journal:

▶ Why did I bury this in my Shadow?
▶ How do I feel about it now that I've rediscovered it?
▶ What emotions do I remember feeling at the time I chose to bury this thing in my Shadow?
▶ What physical sensations do I remember experiencing at the time?
▶ If I could go back to the moment I buried it, what might I do to show more compassion to myself and my Shadow?
▶ Under what circumstances might I feel compelled to bury this feeling, desire, impulse or experience again?

Once you've worked through these prompts for each item on your list, set your timer for 10 minutes and reflect on these questions.

▶ When I review the reasons I buried parts of me in my Shadow, what patterns and similarities emerge?

▶ How can my Shadow and I work together to manage the things that trigger me?

Set off Shadow joy

In this exercise, you've focused on identifying what sets you off so that you can avoid forcing your Shadow to swallow your most difficult feelings. But it's important to remember that not all experiences trigger shame, pain or anger. Some experiences, desires, feelings and impulses can trigger joy.

It is just as important to pay attention to what makes you feel happy and fulfilled, so before you move on with your day, take a moment to jot down a few notes in your journal about the last time you felt joyfully validated. What experiences triggered you to feel confident, secure, safe, exuberant, *yourself*?

If you need help triggering a little joy, you can turn to any of the Shadow Self-Care strategies that you've resonated with in this book so far.

And, when you feel ready, return to this book for the next step on your Shadow Path.

EXERCISE TWO: SHADOW SCAN

In this somatic exercise, you're going to practise a body-scanning exercise that will help you see your Shadow as a safe place for you to draw strength from, instead of using it as a hiding place for your difficult experiences.

A body-scan exercise is a mindfulness technique that combines visualization with sensory engagement. It's a common tactic in somatic therapy, and has been proven to reduce stress, increase awareness and de-escalate difficult emotions.

You know already that practising somatic techniques as part of your Shadow Work can help create new pathways for healing. In today's exercise, you're going to learn a technique that you can use and adapt whenever you feel triggered or at odds with your Shadow instead of working in partnership with it.

Before you begin, take a moment to reflect back on your notes from the last exercise. Refamiliarize yourself with what you wrote about the physical sensations you experience when you feel triggered by shame, anger, fear or other difficult emotions. Choose one of those sensations and imagine what sensation would soothe it. For example, if anger makes you feel hot, then the soothing sensation might be a cooling breeze; if anxiety makes your chest tight, then the soothing sensation might be cool, open air; if fear is slick and slimy to you, what soothes it might be soft, dry and warm.

You will need
- A quiet, peaceful place where you can sit, or lie down without being disturbed
- A timer
- 20–30 minutes of your time
- Your journal and something to write with

Meditation to explore your triggers

Once you have your soothing sensation in your mind, go ahead and read through the following meditation before closing your eyes and trying it for yourself. You don't need to memorize the entire journey; simply read through to get a sense of the content and then lead yourself through the major points, staying open to where your own mind and soul take you.

Set the timer for 10 minutes.

Begin by taking several deep breaths, allowing yourself to settle into the body and the present moment.

When you feel ready, close your eyes and continue taking deep breaths.

After a moment, concentrate your attention on the soles of your feet, and let it slowly move upwards through your ankles, your calves, your knees, thighs, hips, seat, belly, ribs, arms, chest and back, neck, face, and crown of your head.

Return your attention to your feet and repeat the scan,

only this time, as you guide your attention through the body, imagine that what's moving through you is your Shadow.

Return your attention to your feet one more time, and let your Shadow move through you once again, but this time imagine that as it moves through you, your Shadow is filling you up with the soothing sensation you reflected on before you closed your eyes. Welcome this gesture as an act of care and love from your Shadow. Trust that this soothing touch comes from a well within your own depths, a medicine your Shadow has been desperate to offer you all your life, if only you would allow yourself to feel it.

When you are flooded with that soothing feeling, imagine yourself overflowing with it. Picture it filling the room around you, the building you're in, the street you're on, the town, the country, the planet. Picture yourself rising with the tide of it, floating on this infinite source of wellbeing. Your Shadow and your depths, once a dark unknown, now the support beneath your body, holding you.

Float there for as long as you need, and when you're ready allow your eyes to open.

Now, reach for your journal, and record how that went for you.

▶ How did it feel to connect with your body and your Shadow through this exercise?
▶ What physical sensations did you experience?
▶ How could you adapt this body-scan exercise for future use?

Shadow wellspring

You don't need to be in distress to use this exercise; in fact, practising it when you feel calm and grounded can help make it more effective when you do face challenging moments. If you can, try to incorporate it into your regular pre- or post-Shadow-exploration routine for the rest of your journey down the Shadow Path.

If you don't have time for the whole thing, simply take three deep breaths while picturing yourself in the final image of the meditation – floating, supported by your Shadow's soothing presence.

If you need extra soothing beyond today's exercise, try referring back to one or more of the Shadow Self-Care tips from previous chapters.

And, when you feel ready, return to this book for the next step on your Shadow Path.

EXERCISE THREE: SHADOW FIRST AID

In this exercise, you'll build a kit of comfort items you can turn to to help you and your Shadow regulate when challenging experiences threaten your shared progress.

If you have any children in your life – or if you can remember being a child – you'll know all about the drama of visiting the doctor for a shot. You may also know the secrets to winning most kids over after the minor trauma of a needle – think cheery, colourful plasters and lollipops.

This simple aftercare achieves several important things on these little ones' healing journeys: applying a plaster acknowledges, validates and treats their pain, while offering a choice of different colours or characters returns some autonomy to them. Combine that colourful new body decor with a sugary treat and you've transformed a traumatic experience into a novel one. When you conclude a scary experience with generosity, kindness and genuine validation, it goes a long way in softening the blow of the ordeal without sweeping it under the rug.

When you think about it, caring for yourself when you're triggered isn't so different to soothing a child after a shot. You need your feelings to be validated, acknowledged, treated. You need autonomy. You need to temper the scary experience with sweetness, so that it doesn't morph into trauma you want to hide away.

This exercise is all about building a kit of comfort items – the equivalent of those colourful plasters and lollipops – that can help you validate your pain, reclaim your autonomy and treat yourself. Consider it a Shadow first aid kit that you can turn to any time you need a little extra boost to help you manage the discomfort of processing tough emotions instead of hiding them under the floorboards of your soul.

My personal Shadow first aid kit includes the following: my softest pair of socks, fizzy candy, a fidget toy, tea bags, my tarot deck, a cooling eye mask and a couple of books I love to re-read. I also cut out a photo of a bathtub from a magazine and taped it to the lid to remind me that taking a hot bath or shower always makes me feel better! Whenever I'm emotionally overwhelmed and in danger of acting in a way I may regret (or carelessly asking my Shadow to carry the load instead of me), I encourage myself to dig around inside the kit and choose an item or two to engage with as mindfully as possible. I try to take in the sensory comfort and/or pleasure they offer and I invite my Shadow to enjoy it with me.

You will need
- At least 1 hour of your time
- A basket, box or tote
- Meaningful comfort items for your kit
- Your journal and something to write with

Create your own Shadow first aid kit

First, in your journal make a list of items you think can offer you comfort and joy when you're facing challenging emotions or impulses. Focus on things that soothe or please your senses: think pleasurable textures, scents, flavours and colours. Ask your Shadow if it has any ideas.

Next, choose an empty box, basket or tote to hold the contents of your Shadow first aid kit.

Put any comfort items that you already have inside.

If there are any items you'd like to source, set a budget you're comfortable with and do some shopping. Examples might include a soothing face mask, a weighted blanket and an aromatherapy diffuser. Once you have them, add these items to your first aid kit.

When it's full, take some time to get comfortable with what's inside your kit. Explore the way the items you've chosen engage your senses. Reflect on how they make you feel and what makes them soothing for you.

Keep your kit somewhere easy to access, so that you can get to it quickly whenever you need it.

Small Shadow pleasures

If this exercise feels a little overindulgent, that's because it is, and that's the point. You spent years depriving yourself of the validation and healing you needed, burying things in your Shadow to survive, and missing out on the opportunity to commune with your depths and experience life as your fullest self.

By creating a kit of small pleasures that can help you reframe how you respond to difficult emotions, you're actually doing valuable Shadow Work. You're giving yourself – and by extension, your Shadow – the validation and care that you were taught to withhold.

Take as much time as you need over the next few days to continue getting familiar with your first aid kit, and adding to it as you see fit.

And when you feel ready, return to this book for the next step on your Shadow Path.

EXERCISE FOUR: SHADOW VOWS

In this exercise, you'll commit to loving your Shadow. You'll lay out what you need from it, and what it can expect from you.

You learned early on along your Shadow Path, when you named your Shadow, that words have power. And that power isn't just in a name – it's in the commitments that we make. That's why contracts are crucial in business, why lovers write wedding vows, why authors dedicate their books and why families agonize over what is written in wills.

What we commit to in writing is like a spell – it manifests our intentions.

Over the course of your journey down the Shadow Path so far, you've begun to explore the benefits of working with your Shadow, what you need from it and what it needs from you, but now it's time to make it official by putting the commitment you've made into writing and legitimizing the bond you've built up until now.

In today's exercise, you'll write a vow of commitment to your Shadow – you'll cast a soothing spell of protection around the two of you with your words and manifest the intentions you have for your relationship with your Shadow moving forward.

You will need
- A peaceful, quiet room
- 30 minutes of your time
- Your journal and something to write with

Write a vow of commitment to your Shadow

Set your timer for 20 minutes and reflect in your journal on the following questions:

▶ What do I appreciate about my Shadow?
▶ What do I rely on my Shadow for?
▶ What do I need from my Shadow?
▶ What could my Shadow do to meet those needs?
▶ What does my Shadow appreciate about me?
▶ What does my Shadow rely on me for?
▶ What does my Shadow need from me?
▶ What can I do to meet those needs?
▶ What kind of life do I want to co-create with my Shadow?
▶ How can my Shadow and I align on that vision?

When the timer goes off, review what you've written and use your answers to draft your Shadow Vows, using the template below:

From this day forward, I trust you, my Shadow, to keep me and my most vulnerable feelings safe. In return, I vow to honour and respect you all of our days.

I know that when I face difficult emotions and experiences, I can count on you to [FILL IN THE BLANK].

I'm confident that my dreams, desires, impulses and secrets are safe in your care, and that you'll nurture the parts of me I'm still learning to embrace, like [FILL IN THE BLANK].

I have faith in our partnership, and I know that when we work together, our life can be [FILL IN THE BLANK].

As my partner in bringing that vision to life, I'm relying on you to [FILL IN THE BLANK].

I know that our shared vision for a more fulfilled life takes commitment from both of us, so I'm dedicated to taking care of you as much as I need you to take care of me.

You can trust me with [FILL IN THE BLANK].

I promise to [FILL IN THE BLANK] and to never [FILL IN THE BLANK].

Shadow ceremony

If you want to deepen this exercise, consider holding a small Shadow Vow ceremony. Light a candle, hold your Shadow Talisman in your hands and read the vow you've written using the template above out loud.

As always, consider taking a moment to practise one or more of the Shadow Self-Care tips from each chapter so far on pp. 29, 53, 81, 104 and 129.

When you feel ready, return to this book for the next step on your Shadow Path.

Week Six Reflection Prompts

This week, you've developed some vital practices for caring for yourself and your Shadow: you've learned to identify what triggers you to misuse your Shadow, equipped yourself with tools and strategies you can lean on in difficult moments and renewed your commitment to working with – not against – your Shadow.

As your sixth week on the Shadow Path comes to a close, set your timer for 15 minutes and reflect back on the week in your journal.

Ask yourself
- What did I discover about my Shadow this week?
- Which exercise from this week taught me the most?
- Which exercise from this week was the most joyful?
- What support and comfort could I benefit from before heading into the next week?

WEEK SEVEN:
FREE YOUR SHADOW

This week, you'll experiment with (safely and responsibly) letting your Shadow loose into the world.

Over the last six weeks, you've learned that we are all societally conditioned to hide parts of ourselves that are deemed too much, too difficult, too uncomfortable. That when we go out into the world, we cloak ourselves in presentability. We project the versions of ourselves that are easy for others to digest, like and predict. We fish the difficult things out of our pockets and leave them on the mantelpiece at home – or at least, we pretend to ourselves and others that we do.

Then, we walk through the world as pale versions of ourselves. We feel unseen, misunderstood, missed out on. We misunderstand and miss out on others, too. Ultimately, all of these missed connections lead us to miss out on experiencing the world as it truly is, because we don't bring ourselves – as we truly are, Shadow and all – to it.

Reclaiming the world with your Shadow is a way of seeing yourself, understanding yourself, completing yourself. Stepping into the world with your Shadow by your side, instead of chained up somewhere you can't reach it, you open the door to feeling connected to, seen and understood by the outside world that you've been conditioned to hide so much of yourself from.

The more comfortable you become with your Shadow's presence in your life, and how it comes into play during your experiences in the world, the more opportunities you'll have to understand yourself from every angle and discover the gifts that are hidden in your depths. You have to open a book and read it if you want to benefit from what's inside. You have to give a plant water and light so it can live. And you have to let your Shadow experience the world if you want it to reveal its mysteries and gifts to you.

Your Shadow used to be a hiding place, but now is the time for it to take its rightful place: beside you, as an honoured and respected part of who you are.

This week, you'll take gentle steps to get comfortable allowing your Shadow out into the world, first by letting it make itself at home in your private space, then by testing the waters of what it feels like to walk into the outside world with your Shadow at your side, and ultimately by exploring what Shadow impulses and desires you might be ready to take action on in your life.

You'll be challenged to own parts of yourself that you once felt ashamed of, or feared, to celebrate your Shadow's presence in your life, and to practise living in a world that you share with your Shadow, instead of depriving your Shadow of light and showing up to your life as only half of yourself.

A note of caution

In charting this new territory with your Shadow, it's important to exercise caution, since it is possible to confuse our Shadow desires with harmful impulses.

Before acting out any previously suppressed desires or impulses, take a moment to consider the consequences your actions may have on others. While it's OK, and very much part of the process, to make room for discomfort and allow yourself to be judged by others for choosing what feels right for you, it's important not to act on any impulses that might result in physical harm to yourself or others. Sometimes acknowledging the thought can be enough to allow yourself to release it, but if you find yourself ruminating on any violent impulses, take a break and tend to yourself using the Shadow first aid kit you created in Week Six (see p. 165), or any of the self-care and self-regulation strategies you've learned to practise over the course of this book so far.

And if any harmful impulses persist, please contact a mental health professional who can safely guide you through processing those feelings.

SHADOW SELF-CARE FOR WEEK SEVEN

This week's exercises are designed to draw out your Shadow more directly than ever before. It can be particularly exhausting work, so take extra care to look after yourself over the next few days.

Make use of the Shadow first aid kit you built last week, and/or try some of the tips below.

Week Seven self-care prompts

▶ Take a day off from everything – including your journey down the Shadow Path – and rest. Watch a favourite film, eat your favourite foods, wear your comfiest clothes and allow for a true retreat from your efforts.

▶ Book a massage or other care treatment for yourself. Putting your body in someone else's hands to be cared for may help you relax and recover from the effort of guiding your Shadow into the world.

▶ Do something kind for someone else. Exploring your hidden and secret impulses can be confronting. Connecting with your altruistic side and making an effort to do something for others can help ground you, remind you of the value you bring to your community and soothe some of the discomfort you may be experiencing as you re-evaluate how you show up to the world.

EXERCISE ONE: SHADOW OUTING

In this field trip exercise, you'll invite your Shadow on a brief, low-pressure adventure into the world.

This week, you are actively making an effort to take your Shadow self out of hiding. To embrace the gift of experiencing the world as your whole self.

If you've been carrying your Shadow Talisman around in your pocket, or wearing it out of the house, you may have already been intuitively experimenting with the principles of this exercise, but today is a little different. You're going to extend an intentional invitation to your Shadow to step out into the world with you, and you're even going to practise letting it take the lead.

It starts with a simple walk around the block.

Before you leave, take some time to prepare yourself and your Shadow for this experience. Speak your intention aloud, or write it down. You might say: 'Today, I'm going to go outside, and I'm bringing my Shadow with me.' Or you might even address your Shadow directly using one of the names you devised for it during the first week of your Shadow Path journey: 'Shadow, today I'm going to go outside. I'd love for you to come along with me.'

Extending this invitation is powerful and important, even if it feels strange in the beginning. And it most likely will feel strange; after all, it's very counter-intuitive.

The truth is, your Shadow rarely receives invitations. It's much more accustomed to rebuffs. After all, for years you kept your Shadow under lock and key like a monster, instead of by your side, like a trusted companion. Only recently have you begun to kindly, respectfully coax it out.

Remember though, that you've forgiven yourself for how you treated your Shadow in the past. The fact that you and your Shadow developed a warden–prisoner dynamic is not your fault; you were likely taught from a young age that elements often associated with Shadow – emotionality, hyperactivity, or nosiness, for example – are inappropriate or unappealing, and that those qualities couldn't be brought out into the world with you. That it was too vulnerable, too weird or too undesirable to share certain natural parts of yourself.

You were *taught* to chain your Shadow up and leave it behind whenever you stepped out into the world. But now, equipped with a new knowledge and respect for your Shadow, you have a chance to correct it, and to intentionally experience the world with your Shadow at your side.

> You will need
> - Shoes and other weather-appropriate clothing
> - 20 minutes of your time
> - Your Shadow Talisman
> - Your journal and something to write with

Take a field trip with your Shadow

When you leave the house, take a route that's familiar to you, but allow yourself to see it in a new light – or a new Shadow. Imagine seeing the world through your Shadow's eyes. What sights, sounds, smells and other sensory experiences generate fear, curiosity, excitement, desire?

Imagine your Shadow walking beside you. What energy is emanating from it? Where does it want to go? Gently indulge your Shadow's curiosity where you feel safe to: if you're drawn to inspect something you notice more closely, or to take an unexpected turn or two, to see where it leads you, honour that message from your Shadow.

Where you don't feel you can indulge your Shadow – if it's sending you too far from home, or you feel unsafe in any way, you can choose to simply acknowledge your Shadow's presence without following its lead. You can say – out loud if you feel comfortable to do so – 'That's an interesting impulse, and I would feel safest exploring it in my journal when I get home, rather than acting it out here now.'

When you get home, reflect on your short but monu-mental excursion with your Shadow. Take your journal and in it record what you noticed, felt and thought about through words and/or sketches. Reflect on where you indulged your Shadow, and where you took the reins back. Consider where you might want to go together next.

One small step for Shadow kind

Trusting yourself, and your Shadow, to step out into the world side-by-side, even if only for a walk around the block, is monumental. This has been an exercise in self-compassion, self-control and self-discovery.

The next time you take a walk – whether you choose to invite your Shadow along or not, take special notice of literal light and shadow as you move; pay attention to the interplay between light and dark. To the movement and relief of shadows and light on surfaces. Reflect on how this dance of light and dark mirrors your experience on your Shadow Path so far.

Before you move on with your day, consider taking a moment to practise one or more of the Week Seven Shadow Self-Care tips on p. 179.

When you feel ready, return to this book for the next step on your Shadow Path.

EXERCISE TWO: TRUTH OR DARE

In this journalling exercise, you'll get brave with your Shadow by exploring its deepest secrets and identifying hidden desires you're ready to act on.

Do you remember playing Truth or Dare as a child or teenager? That rollercoaster of exhilaration and dread as you devised ways of getting beneath your friends' skins while waiting uneasily for your own moment under the microscope?

The way I see it, part of the discomfort and thrill of Truth or Dare has always been that it forces us to access our Shadow and draw what hides there to the surface. It provokes us to reveal our secrets or act out 'wild' behaviours – to expose versions of ourselves that we normally keep under wraps.

Whether by design or by accident, this adolescent sleepover activity serves as a container for pushing the boundaries of what's considered acceptable or appropriate and offers players the chance to live out taboo ideas, or bare shameful secrets within the hopefully safe confines of game play. You might call Truth or Dare a prototype of Shadow Play.

Today, you're going to take yourself back to those daring, exploratory days of your adolescence by playing Truth or Dare once again – this time, with your Shadow.

You will need
- A quiet, peaceful place
- A timer
- 20 minutes of your time in the first instance
- At least 10 minutes of your time every day for the rest of the week
- Index cards or squares of paper
- A jar, box, tote bag or empty drawer
- Your journal and something to write with

Engage yourself in a game of Truth or Dare

Set your timer for 5 minutes. During that time, make a list of all the questions you have for your Shadow. For example: 'What are you most afraid of?' and 'What makes you feel excited?' This is your Truth list.

When the timer goes off, set it for another 5 minutes. Now make a list of things you'd like to do if you didn't feel ashamed. For example:

▶ Dance in public, even though I think I have terrible rhythm.
▶ Ask out that person I think is out of my league.
▶ Talk to my partner about something I'd like to experiment with in the bedroom.
▶ Come out to my parents.

This is your Dare list. Note: exclude any impulses towards violence or cruelty from these desires; while this exercise is designed to help you bring to the surface impulses you'd typically bury, it is not permission to cross other people's boundaries, or do harm to yourself.

Now, copy each Truth and Dare you've generated onto an index card or square of paper. When you're finished, deposit your Truths and Dares into a jar, box, tote bag or empty drawer.

Then, reach in, and choose a card.

If you draw a Truth, set your timer for 10 minutes and journal about your response to the question. Consider how you'd naturally answer it, and then look deeper to uncover what you think your Shadow might say in response to the prompt.

If you draw a Dare, complete the task on it. Do it today, if possible. Otherwise, take a concrete step towards it today. You could set a date in your diary for when you'll take action, purchase an item you'll need to make the Dare happen or ask someone in your life for support or accountability to help you make your desire a reality.

Continue to pull a card – and take action to fulfil the prompt or task – each day this week.

The daring truth

Your Shadow Path has, all along, been one long game of Truth or Dare with yourself. You've admitted to and owned the things you once hid away even from yourself, and you've challenged yourself to open yourself up to new ways of seeing and being in the world. The journey has been – and will continue to be – a courageous and playful adventure, one Shadow Truth and one Shadow Dare at a time.

If the process of writing down your questions and your desires helps you to take action and continue to live life in a way that honours your Shadow, I encourage you to keep the practice up even after you've completed this week on your Shadow Path. Add cards to your Truth and Dare prompt collection as desires and questions strike you and return to these prompts regularly.

After every Shadow Truth or Dare session, reserve time and energy for some self-care. Do what feels right to you or turn to one or more of the Week Seven Shadow Self-Care tips on p. 179.

And, when you feel ready, return to this book for the next step on your Shadow Path.

EXERCISE THREE: SLIDING SHADOWS

In this journalling exercise, you'll plot out the story of what your life might look like if your Shadow was pulling all the strings.

If you've ever wondered what life – what you – might be like if only things were different, if only you'd made different choices, had different choices . . . you're the furthest thing from alone.

Telling ourselves the stories of who we might have been, of what we might have done if things had been different, is an age-old occupation. In fact, it's one of the driving factors behind the human imagination: we ruminate on what could have been as a means of learning from our experiences and reflecting on what we can do better next time.

Popular books and movies have explored all these branching possible versions of us through parallel universe narratives: think of the films *Sliding Doors* and *The Butterfly Effect*, both of which offer a take on how individual lives and loves might have wound up differently if characters had made different choices or encountered different obstacles . . . or Philip K. Dick's classic speculative novel, *The Man in the High Castle*, in which he subverts the outcome of the Second World War and imagines how modern politics would be affected.

Over the past six weeks of getting to know your Shadow and discovering parts of yourself you'd hidden away, you may have begun to build your own Shadow-centric parallel universes inside your head. What might have been – both good and bad – if all the things buried in your Shadow had surfaced sooner, or never had to be hidden away at all?

In this exercise, you're going to indulge your imagination on this front by scripting a fantasy adventure in your own parallel universe: one where your Shadow self has been on the surface with you all along.

> You will need
> - A quiet, peaceful place
> - A timer
> - About 30 minutes of your time
> - Your journal and something to write with

Write your story with your Shadow in charge

Pick up your journal and a pen and set a timer for 30 minutes.

Ask yourself: what would a day in my life look like if my Shadow had always been free? Then, tell yourself that story.

You can doodle frames for a comic, or script out a play, that depicts a day in the life of the person you imagine you might be if you'd never felt pressured to bury parts of yourself in your depths.

When the timer goes off, set another 5 minutes on the clock to reflect on the experience of imagining this version of your life. Consider:

- ▶ What did I learn from my Shadow through this exercise?
- ▶ What elements of the life I imagined do I wish were part of the life I do live now?
- ▶ What small action can I take to bring those elements into my life, now?

The story of your Shadow life

If you'd like to extend this exercise, consider using it as a daily or weekly journalling prompt. Ask yourself these two questions:

- ▶ How might this day or week have been different if my Shadow had been in charge?
- ▶ Do I want to take action to manifest some of those differences in my life for tomorrow/next week?

As always, at the end of this Shadow exploration session, consider taking a moment to practise one or more of the Week Seven Shadow Self-Care tips on p. 179.

When you feel ready, return to this book for the next step on your Shadow Path.

EXERCISE FOUR: SHADOW ALTAR

In this exercise, you'll honour your Shadow by creating a physical space – an altar – in your home where your Shadow is safe to emerge.

Last week, you invited your Shadow into your home as a guest, and this week, you've experienced letting it out into the world. Now, it's time to give it a permanent space of its own by constructing an altar that welcomes and honours it – somewhere it can return to after your adventures together, somewhere it feels safe to call home.

Traditionally, an altar is a ceremonial platform upon which religious rites are performed. The construction and maintenance of altars has been common practice since the dawn of human consciousness. Ancient Greeks and Celtic worshippers placed sacrifices on their altars, Buddhists constructed altars in their temples to protect and honour images of the Buddha, and Christians performed communion rites at an altar. Followers of spiritual traditions from around the world light candles of remembrance and reverence at their altars, and it's globally ubiquitous for marriages to take place at altars.

Altars aren't only fixtures in temples, churches, and other sacred sites. Many traditions – from Hinduism to Roman Catholicism to Wicca – install altars in the home to honour their gods, saints and spirits.

As part of my personal tarot practice, I have an altar space on my office shelf where I place significant cards, reminding me to call in their energy. I know several artists and writers who maintain altars to their creativity: they decorate a small, dedicated space with objects and photos that represent the current project they are working on, or otherwise furnish their altars with art and items that inspire their work.

The truth is, many modern altars are not religious or blatantly spiritual at all: the stages where musicians and actors perform become altars to our love of art and entertainment, even our dedication to certain performers; when we decorate and design our desk space, we create altars to our work; a thoughtfully curated bookshelf can be an altar to a love of stories; a display of photos on the mantle can be an altar to the people, animals and places we love. Even a Pinterest board can be a kind of altar: to our imagination, our goals and dreams, the aesthetics we appreciate.

So, altars don't necessarily require us to worship, but they do draw us to *honour* the subject of the altar. To be present with it. To invite it into our lives and hold physical space for it to exist.

In that spirit, I invite you to construct and maintain a small, thoughtful altar space to your Shadow. Gone are the days when you locked your Shadow away – today, you honour it in the open. You offer this space as a symbol of the respect, care and acceptance you've cultivated for your Shadow over the course of your Shadow Path so far.

You will need
- A quiet, peaceful place
- About 45 minutes of your time
- Objects to display on your altar
- Your journal and something to write with

Make an altar in your home

Note: This exercise must be done at home. Choose a space in your home for your altar and clear it. The space doesn't have to be big – it can be a portion of a bookshelf or dresser. If possible, there should be some regular access to natural light. No matter what, it's essential that your altar is exposed and visible to you – don't hide it away behind a lid or cupboard door or set it up inside a closet. Remember, this exercise is an experiment in honouring your Shadow and bringing it out into the open, not a new method of keeping it out of sight.

Decorate the space with objects and images that represent your Shadow, and your Shadow journey so far. For example, you might place your Shadow Talisman there, along with some of the things you've created in previous exercises, like a copy of Week Six's Shadow Vows, your Shadow trophies from Week Four, or your eclipse art from Week Five. Candles are very common fixtures on all kinds of altars, and because of their symbolic significance when it comes to Shadow, it's a great idea to include a candle or two on your Shadow altar (as long as the space is safe for a live flame).

You can also do some research around meaningful symbols that make you feel connected to your Shadow and incorporate them into your altar decor. On my altar I keep a pinecone, a symbol for the Greek goddess Persephone who is associated with the duality of light and dark.

When it's ready, you can bless the space by lighting a candle, and/or playing a song from your Shadow Soundtrack. Call your Shadow by its name and invite it into the space. Tell it that it is always welcome here. But remember – this is only symbolic. Your Shadow won't leave you behind to inhabit this space; it's always part of you. This space is a gesture, a metaphor for your overall attitude of respect towards, and openness to, your Shadow.

Tend to your Shadow altar

Once you've established your altar, be sure to take care of it. Clean it regularly and replace the items on it as your relationship with your Shadow evolves and changes. Many practitioners of witchcraft tend to their altars each season, refreshing the decor and rededicating themselves to the subject their altar is designed to honour. You might consider a similar schedule.

While you continue through this book, you can try tending to your Shadow altar every week by lighting a candle at the altar as you read through each week's exercises, or intentionally finding a place on the altar for new items you might create.

As always, consider taking a moment to practise one or more of the Week Seven Shadow Self-Care tips on p. 179.

When you feel ready, return to this book for the next step on your Shadow Path.

Week Seven Reflection Prompts

This week you've taken a leap of well-earned faith and allowed your Shadow out into the world: you've dared yourself to act out desires you once hid away in your unconscious, imagined a life lived collaboratively with your Shadow and taken steps to honour your Shadow in your daily life.

As your seventh week on the Shadow Path comes to a close, set your timer for 15 minutes and reflect back on the week in your journal.

Ask yourself
- What did I discover about my Shadow this week?
- Which exercise from this week taught me the most?
- Which exercise from this week was the most joyful?
- What support and comfort could I benefit from before heading into the next week?

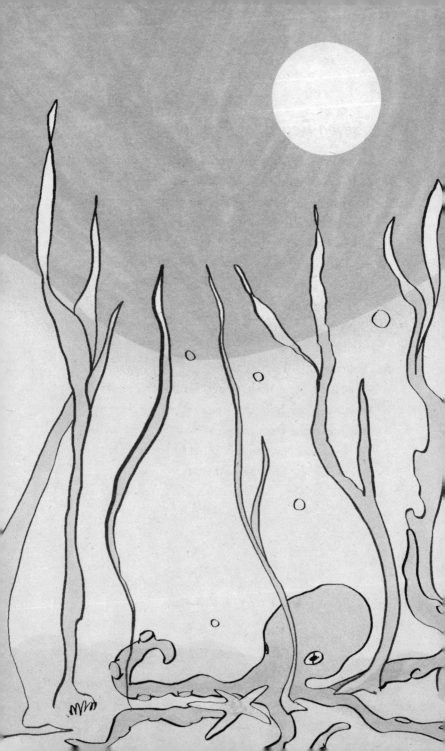

WEEK EIGHT:
DIG INTO YOUR SHADOW

This week, you'll begin to think differently about what it means to bury parts of yourself in Shadow. You'll practise ways to plant comfort, inspiration and peace within your depths.

The once emperor of Rome, Marcus Aurelius, gave himself a command in the pages of his journal: 'Dig inside yourself. Inside there is a spring of goodness ready to gush at any moment if you keep digging.'[10]

Marcus Aurelius was more than an emperor. He was also a Stoic philosopher.

Like Shadow exploration, Stoicism is a widely practised, and yet oft-misunderstood pursuit of self-knowledge and psychological and spiritual resilience. The word 'stoic' is commonly used to refer to someone who shows little or no emotion, someone who seems to have deeply buried all the vulnerable parts of themselves. But the truth about Stoic philosophy has nothing to do with burying our challenging feelings and everything to do with facing our pain head-on so that we can live more peaceful lives. Marcus Aurelius makes it clear: he's digging inside himself to discover the deep wellspring of feeling within, not to bury it.

Like Marcus Aurelius and many Stoics before and after him, you've also committed to digging inside yourself – not just for 'goodness', but for everything that you are.

Over the past two months, you've tunnelled into your Shadow and paved the way for your Shadow to spring forth from your depths, with all the wonders it has to offer in tow. And this week, you'll dig further – breaking new ground, discovering new springs of self-knowledge and potential, and reflecting on the vibrant ecosystem of your own soul.

You'll go to ground and get your hands dirty as you keep tunnelling into yourself. Sometimes you'll find yourself digging for bodies, sometimes you'll find yourself digging for treasure – for Aurelius's 'goodness' – and sometimes, you'll find things you never expected to see at all.

Over the next few days, you'll descend into your depths and practise feeling at home there. You'll uncover remnants of who you once were, and how you want to be remembered in the future. You'll learn how to radically change the way you've approached burying parts of yourself in your Shadow in the past and reflect on what it means to release yourself from difficult experiences, feelings, desires and impulses without neglecting the way they've impacted you. And finally, you'll explore how digging into yourself can be more than just an exploratory mission, but a deeply creative and life-giving experience.

SHADOW SELF-CARE FOR WEEK EIGHT

Since you'll be digging this week, it's a good opportunity to try out grounding practices. Grounding is the process of connecting your spirit or your psyche to the earth by interacting with the natural world.

Try some of these grounding exercises to help you balance the heady digging you'll be doing in your own depths this week:

Week Eight self-care prompts

▶ Go barefoot. Letting your bare feet connect to the ground you walk on is a simple way to ground and deepen your connection to the earth. You can do this inside at home, but the activity is most potent in outdoor spaces. If you have a garden, spend a few minutes standing in it barefoot in the mornings. If not, take a trip to a local park and slip out of your shoes (and socks) for a few minutes to feel your feet on the grass.

▶ Decorate your Shadow altar with plant cuttings or found objects from nature, like stones or fallen leaves.

▶ Eat root vegetables and seeds and reflect on how they connect you to the earth while you chew, taking time to notice the textures, flavours and other sensations.

EXERCISE ONE: SHADOW DESCENT

In this visualization exercise, you'll build on the body scan you learned in Week Six to find an even deeper connection to your Shadow.

Start by reading through the following visualization journey before closing your eyes and trying it for yourself. You don't need to memorize the entire journey, simply read through to get a lie of the land and then lead yourself through the major points, staying open to where your own mind and soul lead you.

I also recommend setting your timer aside for this one, and seeing how it feels to go completely at your own pace.

> You will need
> - A quiet, peaceful place where you can sit undisturbed
> - 15–25 minutes of your time
> - Your journal and something to write with

Visualization to draw on your depths

Begin by sitting in a chair with your feet flat on the floor and taking in several deep breaths. When it feels right, allow your eyes to close.

On your next inhale, imagine that you are breathing in and out from the very top of your head. Focus all your attention on this part of the body as you breathe. Then let your attention move down to your forehead. Breathe in and out from here.

Move your attention down again, to your eyelids, and imagine breathing in and out from here. Do the same for your nose, your cheekbones, your lips, your chin . . . then move your attention further down. Breathe in and out through your shoulders, your elbows, your fingers . . . your collarbone, chest, belly, hips. Follow this pattern all the way down to your feet, moving your attention slowly and intentionally through each part of the body.

When your attention reaches your feet, rest there for several breaths. Imagine your breath entering and leaving the body through your feet.

Then, concentrate your attention specifically on the connection between your feet and the floor beneath you. Breathe specifically into and out from that seam between your body and the floor.

Imagine roots growing from your feet down into the earth, and let your attention move from your body and into these roots.

Draw breath into those roots and breathe out into the earth that surrounds them.

Follow the roots as deep as you can go, breathing into and out from them throughout the descent.

When you feel you're at the deepest point, rest there.

Breathe in and out from this space – the epicentre of your depths. Take in the calm and quiet darkness here and stay for as long as you like.

When you're ready, take a deep breath, drawing all of the energy from this place deep within you.

When you exhale, imagine the breath moving back up through the roots, back up through your feet, up through your body and returning to the crown of your head, where it blooms out of you like a flower.

Draw your attention back to that deep-rooted place once again, breathing in the energy there, and exhaling back up through the body and into that bloom once more.

Do this several more times: draw on your depths, carry what you inhale there up to the surface with your breath and let all that energy and potential bloom out of you as you exhale.

When you feel ready, allow the image of the roots and blooms to fall away, return your breathing to normal, and open your eyes.

Now, reach for your journal, and record what you experienced. Consider these prompts:

▶ How did this exercise make me feel in my body?
▶ How would I describe my roots and the flower that blossomed from them?
▶ How did this exercise help me connect more deeply to myself?

Shadow in bloom

This exercise can be a gentle way of centring yourself and connecting to your depths on days when you don't feel up to the poking, prodding and analysis that often come along with some Shadow Work and Play exercises. Sometimes, it's enough just to stop and smell the Shadow flowers – that is, to appreciate what's there without pushing yourself.

Add this exercise to your growing arsenal of self-care and self-regulation tools and turn to it any time you need to remember the vast power of your depths.

And, if you're in need of some extra care before returning to your day, consider practising one or more of the Week Eight Shadow Self-Care tips on p. 202.

When you feel ready, return to this book for the next step on your Shadow Path.

EXERCISE TWO: SHADOW FOSSILS

In this creative exercise, you'll look to past relics from your Shadow journey so far and fill in the gaps of your knowledge.

A fossil is a remnant of something that used to be alive. Something that was buried, forgotten to the sands of time but never completely lost. The organism leaves behind a part of itself, an imprint of its shape or some other trace. Sometimes the fossil is found and takes on a second life as an object of study. Sometimes it just carries on existing, out of sight but never completely out of time.

Charles Darwin relied on fossils as evidence for his theory of evolution. While each fossil on its own is a frozen snapshot in time, a collection of them can tell a story of change, offering vital information about the past as well as the present moment and even the future.

Your Shadow is full of fossilized material that you've been digging up and collecting since you first began your journey down the Shadow Path. The journal entries and creations you've amassed along your journey are snapshot remnants of what you and your Shadow were like at the time.

Today, your job is to browse that growing collection and reflect on what truths it tells you about who you have been and who you are now.

> You will need
> - A quiet, peaceful place
> - At least 30 minutes of your time
> - Your journal and something to write with

Recap and reveal

Return to the entries you made in your Shadow Journal in Week One. Read them over and reflect on them.

Consider what each entry from that first week tells you about who you were then, how you related to your Shadow and what it felt like to be in the early stages of your Shadow Path.

Record what comes up for you in your journal and take time to make note of what may have changed for you – how you and your Shadow may have evolved – since you first began your journey down the Shadow Path two months ago.

Shadow traces

In her memoir, *Downcanyon*, the naturalist and writer Ann Zwinger muses on fossils: 'I pace the shallow sea, walking the time between, reflecting on the type of fossil I'd like to be. I guess I'd like my bones to be replaced by some vivid chert, a red ulna or radius, or maybe preserved as the track of some lug-soled creature locked in the sandstone – how did it walk, what did it eat, and did it love sunshine?'

Now that you've touched base with the fossils of who you and your Shadow once were, take a moment to imagine what imprint the present version of you now might leave behind. What would you like a future version of you to discover about you and your Shadow as you are now, when you come digging one day?

Before you move on with your day, consider taking a moment to practise one or more of the Week Eight Shadow Self-Care tips on p. 202.

When you feel ready, return to this book for the next step on your Shadow Path.

EXERCISE THREE: SHADOW MEMORIAL

This exercise will help you practise seeking closure with your difficult experiences and feelings instead of abandoning them in your Shadow.

You've spent the last seven weeks digging around in your depths, following your Shadow Path like a treasure map and collecting the gold you find along the way.

Now that you've accepted just how much value there is in your Shadow, it's time to take stock of what you keep with you. At this point in your Shadow journey, it's safe to admit that not everything that has resurfaced through your Shadow exploration needs to be carried around all the time – or even ever again. The best thing we can do for some aspects of ourselves is acknowledge them and the impact they left on us, and then say goodbye.

Sometimes, burial is not an act of hiding, but a gesture of closure.

This goes for painful feelings that you shouldn't have to suffer with infinitely, but also for some of the dreams, desires and talents that you hid away in your Shadow. You aren't obligated to pursue every dream you've ever had. What you do owe those dreams, the version of yourself who once held them and the person you are now is kind, compassionate closure and release, rather than shame and hiding.

In the past, you treated your Shadow like an unmarked grave where you hastily and carelessly covered up things you thought the world shouldn't see. Now that you've learned to recognize and honour those parts of yourself, you can choose to bring what you've buried back to life, or you can choose to honour it by releasing it through a decent, respectful burial.

In this exercise, you'll build a new relationship to burying parts of yourself – by being thoughtful about what serves you, and learning to respectfully release the parts of yourself you no longer wish to carry around, instead of unceremoniously abandoning them.

You will need
- A quiet, peaceful place
- 45 minutes of your time
- A timer
- Paper and scissors
- A patch of dirt and a shovel OR a match and heat-proof bowl
- Your journal and something to write with

Conduct a ceremonial burial

First, take your journal and set your timer for 20 minutes. Reflect on what you've learned about yourself and your Shadow since beginning this journey, and ask yourself these questions:

- What rediscovered parts of myself bring me joy?
- What rediscovered parts of myself bring me peace?
- What rediscovered parts of myself am I curious to explore more deeply?
- What rediscovered parts of myself feel aligned to who I am now and what I want for my life?
- What rediscovered parts of myself don't feel aligned to who I am now, or what I want from my life?
- What rediscovered parts of myself concern events from the past that I can't change?
- What rediscovered parts of myself feel too heavy or painful to consciously carry around with me all the time?
- What experiences, feelings, impulses and desires do I feel ready to release myself – and my Shadow – from?

Now, review your answers to the last four questions, and choose one thing you feel ready to release – something you've rediscovered on your Shadow Path but don't feel drawn to investigate further or carry around with you.

On a fresh piece of loose paper, write about the thing you are choosing to release. Be as detailed as possible. Write about your first memories of it, what prompted you to bury it in Shadow in the first place, how it felt to rediscover it through Shadow Work, what you have learned by reconnecting with it and why it's time for you to let it go.

Now, decide how you'll symbolically release what you've written on the paper. If you have access to somewhere private where you can dig, like a garden or even a plant pot, you can opt to tear or fold the paper and bury it in soil. Alternatively, you can choose to cremate it instead. To do this, you'll tear the paper into strips and place them inside your heat-proof bowl. Then, take the bowl outside to a safe place, set fire to the contents, watch until the flames go completely out and then scatter the ashes.

Invite your Shadow to participate in this moment of memorial and release – this is something you're doing together, not something you're subjecting your Shadow to. As you bury or burn what you've written on the paper, re-assure your Shadow that you're grateful for all it did to keep this part of you safe until you were ready to let it go.

Shadow grief

Taking the time to say goodbye can help ease the complicated emotions that come with releasing parts of ourselves that once held incredible potential. But in the same way that grief doesn't shut off after a funeral, you may still find yourself affected by the experience, feeling, desire or impulse that you chose to release in this exercise. It's important to continue to honour it, even though you've let it go, because if you ignore the lingering grief, you risk abandoning that part of you to your Shadow once again. If you feel haunted, share those feelings with your Shadow by writing about what you're experiencing in your Shadow Journal, or use tarot or oracle cards to facilitate a conversation with your Shadow about what you're going through.

Make time, too, for self-care and self-regulation by turning to your Shadow first aid kit (see p. 165), or any of the Week Eight self-care strategies on p. 202.

And when you feel ready, return to this book for the next step on your Shadow Path.

EXERCISE FOUR: SHADOW GARDEN

In this exercise, you'll celebrate the life that grows from the depths you dig into by planting a seed and nurturing it to grow.

In *Man and his Symbols*, Carl Jung observed that the Shadow is more than a landscape where parts of you hide, it's a breeding ground for new parts to grow, too. Jung writes: 'Just as conscious contents can vanish into the unconscious, new contents, which have never yet been conscious, can arise from it.'[11]

Whenever we bury something in the Shadow, we're also planting a seed from which new unknown desires, impulses and feelings can grow. But without any oversight, weeds and pests like negativity and shame can spring up as quickly as beautiful blooms do. Our depths become overgrown and impenetrable, a dark and unlit forest we are hesitant to enter – picture how it felt to peer into your Shadow in the early stages of your Shadow Path journey, with no idea what you might stumble over in the dark.

Now that you're familiar with, and even sometimes at home in, your own depths, you can start to be intentional about what seeds you leave behind in your Shadow. Instead of burying things as a means of avoidance, you can plant seeds of hope, compassion and curiosity. And by continuing to nurture your relationship with your Shadow, you can ensure those seeds grow into healthy crops that represent a new era of collaboration and care between you and your Shadow. Gone are the days when you littered your unconscious depths with all the things about yourself you thought were too ugly to look at. Here is a new order, one which reclaims your depths as a fertile place where all your potential is flourishing, waiting to be drawn to the surface.

This week, you'll perform a small ritual that represents the lifeforce you're ready to cultivate within your Shadow: you're going to plant a seed.

You will need
- At least 1 hour of your time
- A seed you wish to plant. If you don't have one in mind, lemon balm, chamomile and petunias are all relatively no-fuss options that can flourish indoors.
- A pot of good soil
- A piece of paper
- Your journal and something to write with

Plant your Shadow seed

First assemble your materials. If you are an experienced gardener you may already have what you need, but if you're a novice, you may need to source these. Try to visit a local garden centre rather than ordering materials online, so that you can ask for guidance as needed.

Once you have everything you need, inscribe a message of kindness and compassion to your Shadow on your slip of paper. Roll or fold the piece of paper tightly to make it as small as possible, then set it aside.

Now, prepare your pot with soil. Follow the instructions on the seed or soil packet, or seek out an online tutorial about how to successfully prepare a pot with the kind of soil you've chosen to use.

When the soil is packed into your pot, insert your finger, as deep into the soil as you can to make a hole. Take the rolled-up piece of paper with a Shadow message on it and deposit it in the soil, then cover it back up with soil.

Now, following the instructions on your seed packet, plant your seed.

Copy any care instructions down in your journal and follow them over the coming weeks to nurture your plant, and your Shadow message, to life. Record the care tasks you complete and the growth you see in your journal over time.

Growing Shadow

Your first attempt at growing your Shadow garden may or may not be successful. I have no skill with plants whatsoever, and admit I've struggled – and failed – to keep many alive. If your plant dies, don't take it as any kind of negative omen.

Repeat the exercise if it feels right for you, or simply allow yourself to mourn the loss and process any feelings of frustration or disappointment. Choose another way to remind yourself of the potential your Shadow holds for growth: visit public gardens regularly, read about different types of plants and flowers and draw or write poetry inspired by them or donate money to reforestation programs. Don't let any shame or sense of failure detract from the underlying theme of the exercise.

If and when shoots do arise from your seed, take time to admire your handiwork. Spend time with what grows – smell it, touch it, draw or photograph it, and when the plant is sturdy enough, take cuttings and place them on your Shadow altar, or preserve flower petals in the pages of books.

Whether you're mourning what dies or celebrating what grows, pay attention to the feelings that arise through the process of trying to nurture something to life with your Shadow.

As always, turn to your Shadow first aid kit (see p. 165) and any other self-care strategies you've learned throughout this book if you need them.

And when you're ready, come back again for the next step on your Shadow Path.

Week Eight Reflection Prompts

This week you've dug deeper still into your depths: you've reflected on what's still buried within you and what you can learn from it, and reframed what it means to bury parts of yourself.

Now, as your eighth week on the Shadow Path comes to a close, set your timer for 15 minutes and reflect back on the week in your journal.

Ask yourself
- What did I discover about my Shadow this week?
- Which exercise from this week taught me the most?
- Which exercise from this week was the most joyful?
- What support and comfort could I benefit from before heading into the next week?

WEEK NINE:
TELL YOUR SHADOW STORY

This week, you're going to tell yourself the story of your Shadow journey so far and seek out meaning from beloved stories that can help you understand yourself, your Shadow and the world.

n an interview with *LIFE Magazine*, the American writer and civil rights activist James Baldwin mused on the power of stories: 'You think your pain and your heartbreak are unprecedented in the history of the world, but then you read. It was books that taught me that the things that tormented me most were the very things that connected me with all the people who were alive, who had ever been alive.'[12]

Rather than bury his pain and heartbreak in an unconscious place, Baldwin sought out stories of shared experiences to help him understand himself and the world. And he told incredibly compelling stories of his own. In an article for the *New York Times*, he wrote that 'Nothing can be changed unless it is faced'[13] – a rallying cry as true in the grand scheme of his activism as it was in his own personal quest to sit with and honour his challenging emotions and experiences.

Baldwin sought out stories to make himself feel less alone. He told stories that confronted those things that tormented him – injustice, loss, heartbreak – so that his readers, in turn, would feel galvanized to face their own pain and commit their visions for a different kind of world to paper.

To engage with your Shadow is to engage with stories – the ones you've been told, the ones you've told yourself, and the ones you want to be a part of, moving forward. In the words of one of Baldwin's contemporaries, Joan Didion: 'We tell ourselves stories in order to live'.[14]

This week, you'll tell yourself stories in order to bring your Shadow to life.

You'll reflect on the narrative patterns that have emerged so far on your Shadow journey, and what you can learn about your journey when you tap into stories that are bigger than you. You'll look to beloved literature to inspire a deeper connection to your Shadow. You'll subvert the stories you thought you knew and you'll plot out the next instalment in your own Shadow story.

SHADOW SELF-CARE FOR WEEK NINE

Baldwin, Didion and so many writers before and after them rightly celebrate the power of stories to help us understand our lives. While you're writing your own Shadow stories this week, make time to indulge your imagination by consuming compelling stories that can help you make sense of your own experiences, and inspire your Shadow journey moving forward.

Week Nine self-care prompts

▶ Re-read a favourite book from your childhood and explore how it connects you to joy and innocence you may have buried in your Shadow.

▶ Practise listening deeply when the people in your life tell you their stories. Look for opportunities to connect with them, to see yourself reflected in their experiences.

▶ Seek out the work of memoirists and essayists who write about experiences and challenges similar to ones you've faced in your own life.

EXERCISE ONE: THE SHADOW WITH A THOUSAND FACES

In this exercise, you'll map the most famous storytelling formula onto your Shadow journey.

You may remember the mythologist Joseph Campbell from Week Four (see p. 110), and you probably know his work even if you don't recognize his name. The Hero's Journey, which Campbell lays out in his book *The Hero with a Thousand Faces* served as the narrative foundation for the first *Star Wars* film and has been cited by authors and screenwriters as a crucial storytelling tool for decades.

It's easy to map almost any major blockbuster or commercial novel onto the Hero's Journey. Not because all of these stories are cheap copies of each other, but because the Hero's Journey is what Campbell refers to as a 'monomyth': a narrative that speaks to deep truths about the human experience.

According to Campbell, the Hero's Journey progresses like this:

1. Our hero's story begins in their ordinary world.
2. An event occurs that invites – or pressures – the hero to make a change, to accept a call to adventure.
3. Out of fear, circumstance or stubbornness, the hero refuses the invitation.

4. Something or someone comes into the hero's life and gives them a new perspective.
5. A combination of that new perspective and rising narrative stakes changes the character's mind. They accept the call to adventure they previously declined.
6. Setting forth on their adventure puts a series of events into motion: the hero faces challenges that tempt them to turn back, meets antagonistic forces that test their strength and is forced to reckon with their own weakness or lack of knowledge.
7. Through surviving the challenges, the hero comes to understand the true nature of their adventure, and the stakes if they turn back or fail.
8. The hero is forced to do something they once thought would be impossible.
9. The hero is transformed by achieving this once impossible feat.
10. The hero is called back to their ordinary life, to share the power and knowledge they have gained on their adventure.
11. On the road back home, the hero is unexpectedly challenged once more, by something they thought they had already defeated.
12. They fight to overcome this challenge, and are once again transformed by the experience.
13. The hero makes it back home, changed forever, and shares the wisdom they gained with their community.

If this story sounds familiar, and not just because you've seen it in films, it's probably because it lines up just about perfectly with the trajectory of your Shadow Path journey.

Consider today's exercise a mini call to adventure you can't refuse: I invite you to make yourself the hero of your own Shadow journey by reflecting on how each of the steps above correlate to your Shadow experience.

You will need
- A quiet, peaceful place
- 45 minutes of your time
- Your journal and something to write with

Write your own Hero's Journey narrative

In your journal, work through the steps of the Hero's Journey one by one. Consider how each phase of the narrative reflects your experience on the Shadow Path so far.

When you get to the later stages that you may not feel you have answers for yet, use your imagination to bring your Shadow story to a compelling conclusion. How do you *want* to see this story end?

Changing the Shadow narrative

If you're interested in other ways you might imagine the

points along the map of your own Shadow story, Maureen Murdoch's book *The Heroine's Journey: Woman's Quest for Wholeness* offers a brilliant and feminist take on the Hero's Journey, while Rachel Pollack's seminal text on the Tarot, *Seventy-Eight Degrees of Wisdom*, can help you to shed the baggage of 'hero' and chart your life story along the Fool's Journey instead.

As always when you finish an exercise, consider taking a moment to practise one or more of the Week Nine Shadow Self-Care tips on p. 224.

And when you feel ready, return to this book for the next step on your Shadow Path.

EXERCISE TWO: A SHADOW CAROL

In this creative exercise, you'll riff on a literary classic and explore the ghosts of your Shadow's past, present and future.

In Charles Dickens' classic story, *A Christmas Carol*, Ebenezer Scrooge, a jaded and greedy old man, is visited by three spirits who take him on an adventure through Christmas Eves in the past, present and future.

Over the course of the story, Scrooge reconnects with a past version of himself, reflects on how burying the grief and hurt he experienced in his youth cut him off from his humanity, and ultimately changes his future by acknowledging his pain and reclaiming the kinder, more compassionate parts of himself he lost touch with.

If that's not a Shadow story, I don't know what is.

Today, your task is to create three paintings or collages to represent three spirits of your own: Your Shadow Past, Your Shadow Present, Your Shadow Future.

Your Shadow portraits don't need to be art-gallery worthy. Let this be an exploration in conceptualizing and documenting the different points along your Shadow journey so far. This exercise is staunchly in the Shadow Play camp, so the most important thing to remember is to have fun! Give yourself and your Shadow permission to experiment, to be silly, to *play*.

Don't be afraid to look back to past entries in your Shadow

Journal, or even to directly address your Shadow and ask it how it thinks you should portray it.

You will need
- A quiet, peaceful place
- About an hour of your time
- Art supplies including any of the following: markers, coloured pencils, paints, collage materials
- Your journal and something to write with

Illustrate your Shadow Past, Present and Future

To illustrate your Shadow Past, think back to the very beginning of your journey down the Shadow Path. Try to recall what you knew about your Shadow in those early days and create a portrait that imagines what you saw in your mind's eye then.

To illustrate your Shadow Present, reflect on everything you know about your Shadow right now. Don't worry about making your piece of art cohesive, instead, go for maximalism. Try to include as many details – no matter how conflicting – as possible.

Finally, to illustrate your Shadow Future, challenge yourself to make a piece of art that represents everything you don't know. About yourself, about your Shadow, about how you'll grow together. If you have visions and expectations about where your Shadow Path will lead you going forward, feel free to include them, but don't limit yourself to your ideas of what *will* happen. Embrace, and try to capture, the mystery.

Honour Shadow in your heart

At the conclusion of *A Christmas Carol*, Scrooge sets an intention for the rest of his days, saying: 'I will honour Christmas in my heart, and try to keep it all the year. I will live in the Past, the Present and the Future. The Spirits of all Three shall strive within me. I will not shut out the lessons that they teach!'[15]

In the same spirit, look upon your illustrations, reflect on the lessons you've learned along this journey, and all the things you still want to know. Commit to honouring your Shadow in your heart, long after you've closed this book for the day.

And when you're ready, come back again for the next step on your Shadow Path.

EXERCISE THREE: ONCE UPON A SHADOW

In this exercise, you'll rewrite your Shadow journey as a fairy tale, and explore the ways you and your Shadow rescue each other.

You're probably familiar with the story of Cinderella, a classic rags-to-riches tale of a neglected and abused young woman who rises above her station for a happily ever after life when a glass slipper reveals her to be a prince's true love. You're probably also aware that the sanitized version you've known since you were a child is only half the story: in the version first recorded by the Grimm brothers, Cinderella's stepsisters slice off their toes and heels in an attempt to prove the slipper belongs to them. In an Italian rendition of the story, the Cinderella figure murders her stepmother, and cannibalism appears in some international iterations of the tale.

Like your Shadow, fairy tales hide hidden depths. They are more than a 'happily ever after' – they can be powerful explorations of visceral human themes like loneliness, pain, envy and rage. And, just like the work you're doing to discover your Shadow, uncovering the complex, sometimes dark themes hiding in fairy tales can be an uncomfortable, but ultimately valuable, compelling and inspiring project. Returning to childhood favourites to discover new depths can be healing, revealing, creatively invigorating.

Reclaiming the depths of these stories can be a proxy for Shadow Work and Play. When you draw the hidden complexities and 'unsavoury' or even violent aspects of the tales out of the dark places that the modern sanitized versions have banished them to, you may recognize how powerful it can be to do the same with the stories you've told yourself about your own life.

The past twenty years have seen a rise in fairy tale retellings from the villain's point of view. *Maleficent*, *Cruella*, *Wicked*: these stories all give a voice to the 'dark' side of the pristine fairy tales we're most familiar with, and ask an important question: what if, behind the darkness, hope and beauty lie dormant, waiting to be recovered?

Nothing is all good or all bad. Fairy tales spun by deft tellers to curious readers and listeners know it well: everything has layers and secrets, even the picture-perfect princess who sings to the birds. And everything has beauty hidden within it, even the bitter witch.

In the opening of this book, I quoted from Rainer Maria Rilke's *Letters to a Young Poet*. In the passage, Rilke muses about the true nature of the things that frighten us. He wonders if it's possible that the dragons in our lives are really just damsels waiting for us to rescue them. He begs the question: what if we retold the stories we've been telling ourselves from a different perspective?[16]

In today's exercise, you'll retell a story from your own life, in which your Shadow becomes something in need of saving, and you become its rescuer.

You will need
- A quiet, peaceful place
- About 30 minutes of your time
- A timer
- Your journal and something to write with

Here's what you're going to do:

Set your timer for 5 minutes and brainstorm in your journal about an experience from your past you wish you could have rescued your Shadow – and maybe also yourself – from. Think back to:

▶ Moments when you were made to feel ashamed of something you loved.

▶ A time when you felt hurt and opted to bury the experience instead of soothing yourself with kind words and self-care.

▶ A moment when you accepted bad treatment rather than stand up for your own needs.

When the timer goes off, choose one incident to focus on in this exercise.

Then, tell yourself the story in the format of a fairy tale. Start with 'Once Upon a Time', and go from there. Don't shy away from the difficult parts of the story but do make one crucial change: cast yourself as the character that comes to your Shadow's rescue, its chance for a happily ever after.

Happily ever Shadow

In life, there's really no such thing as a happily ever after, because our lives are not static. There's no freeze-frame end-point after which nothing ever goes wrong ever again. There's only living, there's only trying.

But you can choose to keep creating happy moments with your Shadow, over and over again, over the course of your life, by showing up to rescue it and yourself every day.

As always, turn to your Shadow first aid kit (see p. 165) and any other self-care strategies you've learned throughout this book if you need them.

And when you're ready, return for the next step on your Shadow Path.

EXERCISE FOUR: SHADOW SEQUEL

In this exercise, you'll imagine the continuation of your Shadow Path after your journey with this book comes to an end.

Next week, you'll enter your final week of exercises on your Shadow Path, so it's time to start thinking about what's next . . . to start plotting the continuation of your Shadow journey. A Shadow sequel, if you will.

In modern entertainment, sequels often risk being disappointing. They lack the magic of the original, or just rehash old ground instead of prompting beloved characters to grow and change. Director Francis Ford Coppola derided them as lazy cash grabs, and plenty of famous actors have gone on record to say they prefer to pursue fresh roles instead of getting locked into sequels.

But the continuation of your Shadow story is for your consumption only. You and your Shadow are the directors, the actors, the audience. This story is yours alone. You get to tell it however you damn well please, and you get to rewrite it as many times as you need to in order to find the narrative that helps you move forward.

You will need
- A quiet, peaceful place
- About 30 minutes of your time
- A timer
- Your journal and something to write with

Write your Shadow story sequel

Set your timer for 10 minutes, and work through the following prompts:

▶ What questions about my Shadow do I still want to answer?

▶ How do I want to deepen my relationship with my Shadow?

▶ What new challenges might I need to overcome to take the next journey on my Shadow Path?

▶ What elements of my Shadow Path experience so far do I want to bring with me on the next phase of my journey?

When the timer goes off, use your answers to these questions to chart out your own personal Shadow Path: Part II. Map out a new four-week adventure for yourself, that uses the strategies and knowledge you've gained over the last nine weeks to help you carry on exploring and evolving with your Shadow.

Once you've come to the end of this book's ten-week journey, you can return to this plan and pick up where you left off, but this time, following a path you've written for yourself.

The never-ending Shadow story

Sequels are tricky to get right because the stories we consume as entertainment are meant to end, to come to a close with a neat, satisfying conclusion. But life is different – our story continues for as long as we are alive. There're no such thing as neat endings, just new forks in the road.

Your job is to keep writing your Shadow story, because if it ends, you just wind up back at the beginning . . . separated from your Shadow and unaware of all the stories, all the potential, all the meaning locked inside of it.

As always, turn to your Shadow first aid kit (see p. 165) and any other self-care strategies you've learned throughout this book if you need them.

And when you're ready, come back again for the final chapter on your original Shadow Path.

Week Nine Reflection Prompts

This week you've examined the stories you've told yourself about your Shadow and reinvented the narrative for the next steps along your Shadow journey.

Now, as your ninth week on the Shadow Path comes to a close, set your timer for 15 minutes and reflect back on the week in your journal.

Ask yourself
- What did I discover about my Shadow this week?
- Which exercise from this week taught me the most?
- Which exercise from this week was the most joyful?
- What support and comfort could I benefit from before heading into the next week?

WEEK TEN:
REDISCOVER YOUR SHADOW

In this final week, you'll look back on your ten weeks of Shadow Work and Play by revisiting prompts from earlier weeks to track your growth, evolution and healing.

Ten weeks ago you met your Shadow, and every week since, you've wandered further into your depths, seeking out the treasures and the wisdom hidden away inside you.

And oh, the wonders you've found: hidden joys, creative inspiration, buried strengths, healing comfort and overdue self-acceptance. You've faced demons, too: confronted your fears, your insecurities, your bad habits. You've forgiven yourself and your Shadow and learned to walk confidently into the dark spaces inside you, to look for treasure worth saving and wounds in need of healing.

And yet, after all that, you might wonder why, even as this book comes to a close, you're not out of the woods yet. Why discovering your Shadow hasn't given you all the answers or opened every door.

This is because this Shadow Path is not a straight line. You aren't finished.

It's not a cycle, either. You're not quite back where you started.

This Path is a spiral: you've followed it further than you've ever gone before, but it keeps going.

Writing about spirals and their relationship to understanding and integrating the unconscious parts of ourselves, Carl Jung said that 'the way to the goal seems chaotic and interminable at first, and only gradually do the signs increase that it is leading anywhere. The way is not straight but appears to go round in circles. More accurate knowledge has proved it to go in spirals.'[17]

Later, Jungian scholar William McGuire would summarize Jung's thinking on spirals: 'When you make a spiral you always come over the same point where you have been before, but never really the same; it is above or below, inside, outside, so it means growth'.[18]

To discover your Shadow, to take the risk of delving into the unknown territory beneath your own surface is, as Jung points out, 'chaotic and interminable at first.' But when you carry on, following the little breadcrumbs that emerge as you trust your feet to keep walking, the growth follows.

To the untrained walker, a spiral feels like circling the same spot, but every turn is an opportunity for rediscovery. The longer you commit to walking the spiral, the more your perspective will expand, and the more of your Shadow you'll see – up close, and from afar.

This week, as you round a new bend of the spiral, you'll have the chance to look back at where you've been from a distance, experience it from a fresh vantage point, and see just how much you've grown along the path.

You'll revisit past experiences with your Shadow, repeating them with the benefit of experience.

You'll come back over the same point where you were before, but it won't be the same. And neither will you.

SHADOW SELF-CARE FOR WEEK TEN

Many of the self-care practices throughout this book so far have focused on soothing and relaxing yourself amid the upheaval of digging into your depths. But in this final week, it's time to sit back and enjoy the fruits of your labour by planning a celebration of your successful completion of this book.

You deserve to take some time to appreciate your own resilience, commitment and evolution over these past ten weeks, so I encourage you to reserve some time in your diary for celebrating your progress.

You could book yourself a fancy meal out, gift yourself something luxurious, take a day off and do whatever feels fun and joyful for you, or plan a celebration all your own.

EXERCISE ONE: RETRACE THE SHAPE OF YOUR SHADOW

In this visualization exercise, you'll revisit your very first step on the Shadow Path. You'll reflect on what truths remain, and on how your understanding of yourself and your Shadow have deepened over these past ten weeks.

Start by reading through the following visualization journey before closing your eyes and trying it for yourself. You don't need to memorize the entire journey, simply read through to get a lie of the land, and then lead yourself through the major points, staying open to where your own mind and soul lead you.

If you're more comfortable following the script exactly, you can journal your way through this exercise instead of doing it with eyes closed.

Set the timer for 10 minutes.

Now, are you ready to step back in time, to the moment you first met your Shadow?

You will need
- A quiet, peaceful place where you can sit or lie down undisturbed
- A timer
- 25 minutes of your time
- Your journal and something to write with

RETURN TO YOUR FIRST SHADOW SIGHTING

Allow your eyes to drift over the room that you're in and take in the space around you. Notice the interplay of shadow and light. Is the light warm or cold? Natural or artificial? Where do you notice shadows in the room? What shape and qualities do these shadows take on? How do you feel when drawing your attention to them?

Take in every shadow you can see in the room. Trace its outline with your eyes; notice the depth of its darkness and how its shape mirrors and differs from the objects casting it.

When you're ready, allow your eyes to close.

Imagine yourself in a quiet, but public place. A library, perhaps, or a courtyard or park. It's not empty here, but it's not bustling: a few people are milling around, doing their own thing. You might exchange smiles if you pass each other, but otherwise you're all content in companionable silence.

Take in the scene before you in the same way you observed your room before you closed your eyes. Notice the light in this place. What kinds of objects, architecture, flora and fauna does it illuminate? Where do you see pools of shadow, and what elements of the scene are these shadows attached to?

Take in every shadow you can see in this place. Trace its outline with your eyes; notice the depth of its darkness and how its shape mirrors and differs from the objects casting it.

Now, imagine that at a distance your Shadow is in your field of vision and draws your attention away from your task of tracing shadows.

What do you see?

Imagine that from across the divide between you, its eyes rise to meet yours.

Allow yourself a moment to feel everything that passes between you in this look.

When you're ready, return your attention to the place where you are – that courtyard, library or park. To the objects and shadows you traced moments ago. Trace them again now and consider how you feel after this short encounter.

Let the vision of this imagined place start to fall away, object by object, shadow by shadow, until you're in the quiet dark of your own mind.

Allow your eyes to open.

Now, reach for your journal, and record what you saw. Try not to embellish or add, simply report:

▶ What shape did your Shadow take?
▶ What energy did your Shadow project?
▶ What stood out to you, physically, about your Shadow?
▶ How did you feel, watching it from a distance?
▶ What else did you experience?
▶ Can you sketch out some version of what you saw?

Compare your answers now to the responses you recorded way back at the beginning of your Shadow Path, and reflect on a few final questions:

- How has my perception of my Shadow changed over these last ten weeks?
- How might the story have continued after my Shadow's eyes met mine?

Your Shadow's familiar face

Over the past ten weeks, your Shadow's face and presence may have become familiar, but that doesn't mean the connection between you holds any less magic and wonder. You can return to this exercise any time you need to reconnect to the sense of wonder and reverence you held for your Shadow in the early stages of this journey. You have unlimited mysteries to solve together, as partners in exploring your depths, so take any chance you can to see each other with fresh eyes – it will spur you on and light your path as you wander ever deeper towards the evolving truth of you.

As always, consider taking a moment to practise one or more of the Week Ten Shadow Self-Care tips offered throughout this book.

When you feel ready, return to this book for the next step on your Shadow Path.

EXERCISE TWO: SHADOW SELFIE GLOW-UP

In this exercise, you'll revisit the Shadow Selfie exercise from Week Three, and reflect on how your view of your Shadow and yourself has changed over the last ten weeks.

Almost two months ago, when you were still just getting to know your Shadow, you created a Shadow self-portrait. You were a novice explorer then, still at the edge of the woods. Today, you're a seasoned Shadow veteran; there will be worlds between how you saw yourself and your Shadow then, and how you see it all now.

Today you're going to create a new self-portrait that captures you and your Shadow as you are now.

You will need

- A quiet, peaceful place where you can sit or lie down
- A timer
- At least 45 minutes of your time
- A camera, and/or art supplies such as coloured pencils, pens, paints, clay, collage materials
- Your journal and something to write with
- Optional: costumes, make-up and props

Update your Week Three self-portrait

Start in your journal by brainstorming ideas. Think about what a self-portrait that simultaneously captures you and your Shadow – or that represents you on your Shadow journey so far – might look like. You can jot down notes, start to sketch out your ideas or even use collage materials to make a moodboard. Think about what medium you might like to use – photography, charcoal, watercolour, collage, clay, mixed media?

Consider what props and materials you'll need. Do you want to include certain objects that represent your Shadow, or design a costume or make-up that helps you express your vision?

Then, gather your materials and props, and get to work making your Shadow self-portrait. Don't be afraid to experiment and feel encouraged to check in with yourself throughout.

When you have finished, take out the original portrait you created in Week Three and compare these works of art side-by-side. What changes do you notice? What similarities? What can you see more clearly now, as a Shadow veteran, that you didn't see months ago? And what are you surprised to still recognize in that old version of you, even though it feels worlds away?

Shadow yearbook

If you found this exercise useful and creatively inspiring, I encourage you to keep it up long after you turn the final page of this book. Set a regular date to create Shadow self-portraits – new moons, the anniversary of starting your Shadow Path, or notable astrological dates like equinoxes or eclipses can be good markers.

As always, consider taking a moment to practise one or more of the Week Ten Shadow Self-Care tips offered throughout this book.

When you feel ready, return to this book for the next step on your Shadow Path.

EXERCISE THREE: SHADOW SÉANCE

In this exercise, you'll return to your divination tools from Week Four and your Shadow spirit illustrations from Week Nine to facilitate a conversation with your Shadow about the past, present and future of your Shadow Path journey.

Last week, you created three illustrations to represent different versions of your Shadow, inspired by Charles Dickens' *A Christmas Carol*. You brought spirits of your Shadow Past, Present and Future to life on paper. Now, you're going to revisit these images and dust off your divination skills in order to have a conversation with each of these Shadow spirits – a kind of Shadow séance.

Past, Present and Future are not only a significant chain of words in Dickens' novella – tarot readers will also recognize this trinity as the most common tarot spread in circulation.

A tarot spread is a series of prompts that assigns specific codes of meaning to the cards you draw out of your deck for a reading. As you might expect, a Past, Present, Future spread calls for three cards: the first card you draw represents the past, the second card represents the present and the third card represents the future.

In this exercise, you're going to invite each of the versions of your Shadow that you illustrated to share a message with you.

Note that while this exercise draws on a common tarot reading practice, you don't need to use a tarot deck to participate in this exercise. Other divination tools, like oracle cards and rune stones, as long as you're confident in reading them, will work fine, though a pendulum *won't* be appropriate for this exercise.

If you don't have any of these tools, you can adapt it to the bibliomancy technique you learned in Week Four (see p. 119). Alternatively, you can use the shuffle function on your favourite music app to match songs rather than cards to each prompt.

You will need
- A quiet, peaceful place
- 45 minutes of your time
- A tarot or oracle deck, a book of poetry and/or your Shadow playlist
- Your journal and something to write with

Invite your Shadow to 'message' you

Take your tarot deck (or other tool), your journal, a pen and the illustrations you created in the Shadow Carol exercise (p. 229). Place all of these items on or near your Shadow altar, and light a candle if it's safe to do so.

Start by training your attention on the Shadow Past illustration while shuffling your deck, flipping through your book or shuffling through your playlist. As you shuffle, ask the illustration out loud: 'What do you want me to know?' Then, draw a card, choose a page or hit play.

Take in the card, writing or song that you've landed on, and ask yourself the following questions, writing the answers in your journal:

▶ What do I think my Shadow is trying to tell me?
▶ How do I feel about the card/words/song I'm taking in?
▶ How can I honour this message?

Repeat this process for each of the remaining two illustrations – Present and Future.

Once you've reflected on all three messages individually, take in the reading as a whole. Ask yourself:

▶ What patterns have emerged through these messages?
▶ What elements of this reading resonate with me the most?
▶ How can my Shadow and I move forward together now?
▶ Do I have any follow-up questions that I want to ask by pulling another card/flipping to another page/ playing another song?

When you finish your reading, arrange your Shadow illustrations and the cards you drew on your altar, thank your Shadow for sharing and blow out the candle to bring the 'séance' to a close.

Shadow date night

You don't have to ritualize every conversation you have with your Shadow, but putting effort into the time you spend with your Shadow will go a long way in sustaining a strong, meaningful bond – your Shadow is recovering from a lifetime of being ignored; it needs and deserves some special treatment. Think of rituals like this Shadow séance as special date nights with your Shadow.

If you're feeling at all dysregulated or otherwise vulnerable after your séance, be sure to conduct some Shadow self-care – turn to your Shadow first aid kit (see p. 165), or to any of the Week Ten Shadow Self-Care suggestions offered throughout this book.

And when you're ready, return to this book for the final step of your Shadow Path.

EXERCISE FOUR: SHADOW MEMOIR

In this final exercise, you'll retrace every step you took on your Shadow Path, crossing back over the road you've walked and seeing it all with fresh, wiser eyes.

For this final exercise on your Shadow Path, your task is to keep the memories and lessons you learned along the way alive in your consciousness, and to celebrate just how far you've come since you opened this book ten weeks ago.

Your job is simple: you're going to read your Shadow Journal from cover to cover.

This is a show of reverence for your Shadow. It's an act of love for who you've been and who you've become over the past ten weeks. It's a statement of intent for the next steps of your journey with your Shadow.

So often when we undergo transformative experiences, we don't take the time afterwards to properly process them. Over time, we lose the wisdom and the growth we gained. We backslide. We let some of the most important lessons we learned lapse back into the unconscious, all because we didn't take time to honour the journey by reflecting deeply on what we experienced. Re-reading your journal subverts this pattern and cements your commitment to truly embracing your Shadow and integrating its presence into your life long term.

Besides, you put so much effort into keeping this record

– you deserve to give it the respect of your full attention. To retrace your history, reflect on it, marvel at it, learn from it. To dig into your recent past and shine a light on all of the places you've been, rather than letting your records fade into obscurity . . . slip back into Shadow.

Take all the time you need to complete this final exercise – it will probably take longer than a week. Make notes and annotations as it feels right – use a different-coloured pen, so that you can distinguish between your original entries and your notes.

You will need
- A quiet, peaceful place
- This exercise has no time limit – it takes as long as it takes
- Your journal and a pen in a different colour to your usual one

Dear reader

Read your Shadow Journal cover to cover.

Once you've read your Shadow Journal cover to cover, close out this exercise by allowing your Shadow to speak. Simply take your pen and commit whatever stream of consciousness thoughts arise to paper.

You don't have to read this final entry back – save it for

a future version of you, who will come back to this journal one day with lanterns, looking for yourself.

As always, consider turning to any of the self-care practices you've learned throughout this book to help you re-regulate before getting back to your day.

And when you're ready . . . take whatever next steps feel right for you.

Week Ten Reflection Prompts

Over the past ten weeks, you have ventured deep into the depths of your soul, uncovering hidden truths and treasures hiding in your Shadow.

You've met the other half of yourself and welcomed it into your life.

You've learned to treat your Shadow as a trusted companion rather than a suspicious interloper.

You've come to accept and honour yourself, Shadow and all.

You've interrogated the stories you've told yourself about what you're allowed to do and who you're allowed to be, and opened yourself up to new, exciting, glittering possibilities.

You've prioritized caring for yourself through challenging experiences, and learned to be resilient when you're confronted with difficult feelings and desires.

You've teamed up with your Shadow to make art, to dream dreams, to take risks and to create a loving environment where you can flourish together.

You've reimagined yourself, with a fuller view of everything you're capable of.

And you've come out the other side something wholly new, ready to face the world instead of hiding your most vulnerable – and valuable – parts away from it.

You've found the missing parts of yourself, and through that discovery, you've found new direction.

Now, as your final week on the Shadow Path comes to a close, set your timer for 20 minutes and reflect back on these past ten weeks in your journal.

Ask yourself
- What did I discover about my Shadow on this journey?
- How have I changed for the better over these past ten weeks?
- What has meeting my Shadow freed me to do?
- Which exercise from these past ten weeks taught me the most?
- Which exercise from these past ten weeks was the most joyful?
- What is the next step for me on my own Shadow Path?
- What promises do I want to make to myself and my Shadow moving forward?

NEXT STEPS

Your Shadow Path is yours to chart now. But, in case you need a nudge forward, here are a few things you can do to continue to develop your relationship with your Shadow now that you've completed this book.

▶ Keep your shadow journalling habit going. Consider asking your Shadow a new question each day. Invent your own or turn to p. 271 to find an entire year's worth of Shadow journalling prompts.

▶ Read widely about 'Shadow' to dive even deeper. I've included a Further Reading section on p. 269.

▶ Return to and repeat exercises in this book that you found particularly compelling and/or challenging. You can even repeat this entire program every now and then – once every year or two, say – to help you reconnect to your Shadow as needed.

▶ Experiment with creating your own exercises and prompts – think about what you personally need and want to explore through Shadow Work and Play, and design bespoke practices for yourself that meet your needs in the moment.

▶ Work with a certified Shadow Work practitioner. You can get in touch about working with me at pipcardstarot.com

▶ Most importantly, listen to and trust yourself. Pay

attention to what feels right for you and refer back
to your own writing in your Shadow Journal,
allowing it to reveal what might be next for you.

AFTERWORD:
SAFE IN THE SHADE

I wrote the earliest lines of this book in the winter, when the days were short, dark and cold; when the moon hung large and heavy over my afternoons. I resented the darkness then – hungry as I was for a drop of sunshine and the soft caress of summer air.

Today, as I reach the finish line, summer has arrived. I'm baking on my balcony, desperate for the clouds to creep over the sun and grant me shade, for the cool edge of a breeze.

I'm thinking about how this seasonal change isn't so different from our journeys down the Shadow Path. At first, the darkness oppresses us, but that's only because we don't know what it can do for us – how it protects us and holds space for us in its cool, safe shade.

I don't know where your Shadow journey will lead you next – I don't know where mine will either, but I know this: somewhere along the Path you've walked so far, you've found your way to your depths. You've reunited with the other half of you. And now you have the power to appreciate the light and the dark within you. To claim the pleasure and clarity that comes with warmth and light, but to know the soothing kiss of shade, too.

I hope that going forward, your Path takes you through a forest at dusk, when the night bleeds into the day and darkness and light rest alongside each other, whispering their way through the leaves of trees, dappling the road ahead of you in a glittering mosaic of light and shade. I hope you keep walking, I hope you keep discovering and I hope you keep your Shadow by your side wherever you go.

NOTES

1. Pippin Mizzi, Chelsey. 'Season of Shadow'. *The Tarot Spreads Yearbook*. pp. 46-75. 2023.

2. Jung, Carl. 'The Spirit in Man, Art and Literature'. *Collected Works, vol. 15*. p.82. 2014 edition.

3. Jung, Carl. 'Two Essays on Analytical Psychology'. *Collected Works of Carl Jung, vol. 7*. p. 21. Originally published 1928.

4. Osbon, Diane K. *Reflections on the Art of Living: A Joseph Campbell Companion*. p. 24. 1995.

5. Wilheim, Richard translation. *I Ching*. p. 11. 1949.

6. Jung, Carl. 'Good and Evil in Analytical Psychology'. *Jung on Evil*. p. 89. 1995.

7. Estes, Clarissa Pinkola. *Women Who Run with the Wolves*, p. 372. 2008.

8. Van der Kolk, Bessel A. *The Body Keeps the Score*, p. 101. 2014.

9. Dillard, Annie. 'Total Eclipse'. First published 1982. Accessed from *The Atlantic*'s archives, 2017. https://

www.theatlantic.com/science/archive/2017/08/annie-dillards-total-eclipse/536148/

10. Aurelius, Marcus. *Meditations*. p.67. Penguin 2006 edition.

11. Jung, Carl. *Man and His Symbols*. p.24. Penguin 2012 edition.

12. Howard, Jane. 'Doom and Glory of Knowing Who You Are'. LIFE Magazine, May 24, 1963. https://books.google.fr/books?id=mEkEAAAAMBAJ&lpg=PA1&dq=Life+Magazine,+May+24,+1963&pg=PA89&redir_esc=y#v=onepage&q=dostoevsky&f=false

13. Baldwin, James. 'As Much Truth as One Can Bear'. 1962. https://www.nytimes.com/1962/01/14/archives/as-much-truth-as-one-can-bear-to-speak-out-about-the-world-as-it-is.html

14. Didion, Joan. *The White Album*. p. 11. 2009 edition.

15. Dickens, Charles. *A Christmas Carol*. p. 13. 1915 edition.

16. Rilke, Rainer Maria. *Letters to a Young Poet*. p. 45. Dover Editions, 2021.

17. Jung, Carl. 'Psychology and Alchemy'. *Collected Works of Carl Jung, vol. 12*. p. 28. Originally published 1953.

18. McGuire, William. *Dream Analysis, Volume 1: Seminars*. p. 100. Originally published 2021.

FURTHER READING

This book quotes directly from, or heavily references the following sources:

A Christmas Carol. Charles Dickens.

Downcanyon. Ann Zwinger.

Letters to a Young Poet. Rainer Maria Rilke (The Eighth Letter).

Man and His Symbols. C.G Jung.

Seventy-Eight Degrees of Wisdom. Rachel Pollack.

Shadow and Evil in Fairy Tales. Marie von Franz.

The Body Keeps the Score. Bessel A. van der Kolk.

The Collected Works of C.G. Jung. C.G. Jung.

The Heroine's Journey: Woman's Quest for Wholeness. Maureen Murdoch.

The Hero with A Thousand Faces. Joseph Campbell.

The Interpretation of Dreams. Sigmund Freud.

Total Eclipse. Annie Dillard.

Women Who Run With the Wolves. Clarissa Pinkola Estes.

For further reading to fuel you as you continue down your Shadow Path, consider the following:

Tarot for Creativity. Chelsey Pippin Mizzi.
The Tarot Spreads Yearbook. Chelsey Pippin Mizzi.
I also recommend the following online publications:
The Artemisian by Alyssa Polizzi (alyssapolizzi.substack.com).
The Shuffle by Chelsey Pippin Mizzi (theshuffle.substack.com).

365 SHADOW JOURNALLING PROMPTS

On the following pages you'll find a collection of 365 journalling prompts to help you continue diving into your depths long after you've finished the last exercise in this book.

Like everything you've faced on your Shadow Path so far, some of these exercises are light-hearted and playful, while some of them will prompt you to confront the more difficult aspects of your Shadow journey.

How and when you use these prompts is up to you. You can answer one a day for the next year, or you can turn to them as and when you need. You can do them in the order in which they're written, or you can jump around to answer the questions that call to you.

I would love it if you'd consider using them as prompts for tarot readings or other divination practices (I actually used tarot cards to devise them!), or you used them to inspire poems, paintings, songs or other works of art. Feel free to share your readings and art with me on Instagram @pipcardstarot.

1. How can I find safety in my Shadow today?
2. What can I draw into the light today?
3. Who in my life brings out my Shadow?
4. What is my Shadow drawn to today?
5. What creative opportunities does my Shadow present to me?
6. What problems can my Shadow help me solve?
7. How is my Shadow challenging me today?
8. What gifts is my Shadow offering me today?
9. What qualities do I admire about my Shadow?
10. What do I still want to learn about my Shadow?
11. What passions are hiding in Shadow?
12. What scares me about my Shadow?
13. What excites me about my Shadow?
14. Who can support me when I'm working through difficult elements of my Shadow?
15. How can I play with my Shadow today?
16. What in my life draws attention to my Shadow?
17. When am I most compelled to ignore my Shadow?
18. How does my Shadow need to be acknowledged today?
19. What talents are hiding in my Shadow?
20. What desires are hiding in my Shadow?
21. What does my Shadow reveal to me through dreams?
22. What elements of my Shadow do I want to be more open to?
23. Do I want to share parts of my Shadow with others?
24. What creative mediums help me connect to my Shadow?

25. How does my Shadow make me feel powerful?
26. How does my Shadow make me feel vulnerable?
27. How am I in conflict with my Shadow?
28. How am I in harmony with my Shadow?
29. What secrets is my Shadow keeping?
30. Where would my Shadow love to go?
31. What sensory experiences help me connect to my Shadow?
32. What colour is my Shadow?
33. During what period of my life have I been most disconnected from my Shadow?
34. During what period of my life have I felt most connected to my Shadow?
35. When did I first feel my Shadow's presence – even if I didn't recognize it for what it was?
36. What places do I associate with Shadow?
37. What emotions do I associate with Shadow?
38. How can my Shadow bring me joy?
39. How can my Shadow bring me peace?
40. What elements of my Shadow do I need to pay attention to right now?
41. What part of me needs acknowledgement and acceptance today?
42. What questions do I have for my Shadow?
43. What dreams does my Shadow have for me?
44. What fears does my Shadow harbour, and how can I acknowledge and soothe them?
45. How does my Shadow support my personal values?

46. What elements of my Shadow challenge my personal values?
47. How do I feel my Shadow in my body?
48. How do I express my Shadow through my body?
49. What can my Shadow reveal to me about love?
50. What can my Shadow reveal to me about pain?
51. What can my Shadow reveal to me about pleasure?
52. What can my Shadow reveal to me about ambition?
53. What can my Shadow reveal to me about grace?
54. What can my Shadow reveal to me about fear?
55. What can my Shadow reveal to me about patience?
56. What can my Shadow reveal to me about passion?
57. What can my Shadow reveal to me about desire?
58. What can my Shadow reveal to me about envy?
59. What can my Shadow reveal to me about power?
60. What can my Shadow reveal to me about acceptance?
61. What can my Shadow reveal to me about creativity?
62. What can my Shadow reveal to me about kindness?
63. What can my Shadow reveal to me about intimacy?
64. What can my Shadow reveal to me about shame?
65. How can I be a more devoted student of my Shadow?
66. How can I make my Shadow feel seen, heard and accepted?
67. What elements of my Shadow do I need to acknowledge and embrace?
68. How does my Shadow make my life harder?

69. How does my Shadow make my life richer?
70. What promises can I make – and keep – to my Shadow?
71. What requests do I have for my Shadow?
72. Have I blamed my Shadow for bad behaviour in the past?
73. What do I wish I understood about my Shadow?
74. How can I show my Shadow that I love and accept it?
75. How can I challenge my Shadow without shutting myself down?
76. What parts of me have I exiled to Shadow?
77. How does judgement – from myself and from others – affect my relationship with my Shadow?
78. When have I felt accepted for my whole self – Shadow and all?
79. When have I felt rejected because of my Shadow?
80. What is the most fascinating thing about my Shadow?
81. How does my Shadow protect me?
82. What does my Shadow need to be protected from?
83. What do I wish I'd known sooner about my Shadow?
84. What does my Shadow reveal to me about innocence?
85. What does my Shadow reveal to me about guilt?
86. What does my Shadow reveal to me about relationships?
87. What dreams have I buried in my Shadow?

88. How has my Shadow obscured my self-worth in the past?
89. How can my Shadow help me illuminate my self-worth today?
90. What does my Shadow reveal to me about survival?
91. What elements of my Shadow am I proud of?
92. What would my Shadow wear to a party?
93. If my Shadow were a film, what would it be?
94. If my Shadow were a fairy tale, what would it be?
95. If my Shadow were a taste, what would it be?
96. If my Shadow were a texture, what would it be?
97. If my Shadow were a song, what would it be?
98. If my shadow were an animal, what would it be?
99. If my Shadow were a mythical creature, what would it be?
100. If my Shadow were to have a pet, what would it be?
101. If my Shadow were a flower, what would it be?
102. If my Shadow were a day of the week, what would it be?
103. If my Shadow were a celebrity, who would it be?
104. If my Shadow were famous, what would it be known for?
105. What classic artist would I commission to paint or sculpt a portrait of my Shadow?
106. What questions do I still have about my Shadow?
107. What era would my Shadow like to live in?
108. How would my Shadow dress itself?
109. What is my Shadow's natural environmental habitat?

110. What creative gifts does my Shadow have to offer?
111. How can I honour my Shadow today?
112. In what way does my Shadow need to be challenged?
113. In what way does my Shadow need to be offered love?
114. What does it mean to be kind to my Shadow?
115. How do I feel when I engage with my Shadow?
116. How do I feel when I neglect my Shadow?
117. How do I feel when I bury something in my Shadow?
118. How do I feel when I put pressure on my Shadow?
119. What's the difference between giving my Shadow space, and neglecting it?
120. How does my Shadow communicate with me?
121. What desires do I want to draw out of my Shadow and into the light?
122. How do I feel when I accept aspects of my Shadow?
123. What affirmation can I give my Shadow today?
124. What is my Shadow's favourite memory?
125. Where would I like to take my Shadow on holiday?
126. What cues tell me that my Shadow needs my attention?
127. What acts of kindness soothe my Shadow?
128. How can I lean on my Shadow in difficult times?
129. How can I be playful with my Shadow today?
130. What good memories have I buried in my Shadow?
131. What does my Shadow have to teach me about my past?

132. What does my Shadow want for the future?

133. Where does my Shadow need healing today?

134. What kind of attention does my Shadow need today?

135. What adventures do I want to embark on with my Shadow?

136. How is my Shadow currently holding me back?

137. How am I currently holding back on my Shadow's desires, talents and gifts?

138. What is my Shadow longing for?

139. What elements of myself do I have a habit of shining a light on, versus what elements do I tend to relegate to Shadow?

140. What can I do to mend my relationship with my Shadow today?

141. How does my Shadow help me grow?

142. What is capturing my Shadow's curiosity today?

143. What bores my Shadow?

144. How does my Shadow experience and express grief?

145. What does my Shadow have to teach me about grief?

146. What does my Shadow grant me freedom from?

147. What truths does my Shadow connect me to?

148. What has my Shadow destroyed?

149. What has my Shadow brought to life/created?

150. What has my Shadow rescued?

151. What does my Shadow want to reveal to me today?

152. How can I celebrate my Shadow today?

153. When/in what circumstance does my Shadow feel like a burden?

154. When/in what circumstance does my Shadow feel like a gift?
155. What is my Shadow's quest?
156. What do I owe to my Shadow?
157. What does my Shadow owe to me?
158. How does my Shadow empower me?
159. How does being in tune with my Shadow help me make decisions?
160. Where am I in conflict with my Shadow?
161. What do I want to change about the way I relate to my Shadow?
162. When is my Shadow dangerous?
163. How can I practise acknowledging my Shadow without letting it take over today?
164. What creative instincts are bubbling up through my Shadow today?
165. What pain does my Shadow need me to acknowledge today?
166. How can I claim the power of my Shadow today?
167. What love can I offer my Shadow today?
168. What love is my Shadow offering me today?
169. What message is my Shadow sending me today?
170. What elements of my Shadow am I choosing to ignore?
171. How does knowing my Shadow help me see the world differently?
172. What does my Shadow have to teach me about community?

173. What can I learn about my Shadow through engaging with my community?
174. How does my Shadow benefit me?
175. What makes my Shadow feel at home?
176. How can I make my Shadow feel safe?
177. What does my Shadow have to teach me about peace?
178. What high is my Shadow chasing?
179. What lesson does my Shadow need to learn?
180. Who can help me continue on my Shadow Path?
181. How has my Shadow shaped my past, present and future?
182. What lesson can my Shadow teach me today?
183. What are my Shadow's most valuable qualities?
184. What does my Shadow value about me?
185. What ambitions have I buried in Shadow?
186. In what ways do I feel confident that I know my Shadow well?
187. What am I only just beginning to understand about my Shadow?
188. How can I build trust with my Shadow?
189. What is my Shadow hiding from me?
190. Have I ever tried to hide anything from my Shadow?
191. How does my Shadow care for me?
192. How do I care for my Shadow?
193. What have I denied my Shadow of?
194. What makes me proud of my Shadow?
195. What does my Shadow take pride in?
196. What haunts my Shadow?

197. What have I been dreaming of lately, and what message from my Shadow might those dreams offer?
198. What do I love about my Shadow?
199. What makes my Shadow unique?
200. What have my Shadow and I co-created together?
201. What can I thank my Shadow for today?
202. What work of art, poetry or literature feels like a message from my Shadow?
203. Do I feel connected or disconnected from my Shadow today?
204. What does taking responsibility for my Shadow look like for me today?
205. How can I make more room for my Shadow to express itself safely?
206. What literal shadows can I see around me right now?
207. If I could sum up my Shadow's best quality in one word, what would it be?
208. What textures, scents, sounds and other sensory experiences help me feel connected to my Shadow?
209. What self-care practice helps me regulate after engaging with my Shadow?
210. When was the moment I first became aware of my Shadow?
211. What was the first thing I ever hid away in my Shadow?
212. With whom do I feel safe sharing Shadow parts of me?
213. What rituals and practices help me connect to my Shadow?

214. What makes me feel safe when I'm engaging with my Shadow?
215. How can I strike a better balance between Shadow Work and Shadow Play?
216. How has my view of my Shadow been evolving lately?
217. How does engaging with my Shadow help me be a better friend, partner or family member?
218. How has my Shadow contributed to my success?
219. How has my Shadow affected my choices?
220. How did my Shadow manifest in my childhood?
221. How did my Shadow manifest in my teenage years?
222. How did becoming an adult affect my Shadow?
223. Has engaging more intentionally with my Shadow affected the way I treat others?
224. Has engaging more intentionally with my Shadow affected the way I treat myself?
225. How does my growing awareness of my Shadow affect the way I approach conflict?
226. What can I do to be gentle with my Shadow today?
227. What do I need from my Shadow right now?
228. What boundaries do I need to set with my Shadow?
229. Where do I need to be vulnerable with my Shadow?
230. Do I need Shadow Work or Shadow Play today?
231. What would I like to tell my Shadow right now?
232. What am I avoiding confronting, and how is that affecting my Shadow?
233. What's my Shadow's most toxic trait?

234. What toxic traits of my own have I buried in my Shadow?

235. How can I pause and connect with my Shadow in this moment?

236. What advice does my Shadow have for me?

237. What advice do I have for my Shadow?

238. What is my Shadow curious about?

239. What am I drawn to explore with my Shadow today?

240. What self-regulation techniques work for me when my Shadow is acting out?

241. What comfort does my Shadow need from me?

242. What hidden parts of me want to come to the surface?

243. What am I resisting in my Shadow Work and Play right now?

244. What energy does my Shadow naturally give off?

245. What gender is my Shadow?

246. How can I be sweet to my Shadow?

247. How does engaging with my Shadow change the way I experience the world?

248. What would I do without my Shadow?

249. What would my Shadow do without me?

250. What does my Shadow want to play with?

251. What does my Shadow want to run from?

252. What does my Shadow believe to be true?

253. What do I know to be true about my Shadow?

254. What lies did I use to believe about my Shadow?

255. What traits does my Shadow admire in me?

256. What do I admire about my Shadow?

257. What would my Shadow do if there were no consequences?

258. How can I give my Shadow a safe outlet for its darkest desires?

259. If my Shadow were a natural phenomenon – like a weather event or other act of God – what would it be and why?

260. How would my Shadow celebrate a birthday?

261. Who in my life fascinates my Shadow the most?

262. What luxury would my Shadow take the most pleasure in?

263. What is my Shadow's favourite taste?

264. What is my Shadow's favourite smell?

265. What is my Shadow's favourite sound?

266. What is my Shadow's favourite texture?

267. What is my Shadow's favourite thing to look at?

268. What sensory experiences would my Shadow prefer to avoid?

269. If I could write my Shadow a love poem, what would I say?

270. If I could offer my Shadow a piece of advice, what would it be?

271. How is my Shadow generous with me?

272. How can I be generous with my Shadow?

273. How am I feeling about my current relationship with my Shadow?

274. What does my Shadow need me to know right now?

275. What do I need from my Shadow right now?

276. What does my Shadow want for our future together?

277. How do I envision my relationship with my Shadow to evolve in the future?

278. What three items would my Shadow take to a desert island?

279. What does my Shadow cherish?

280. What is my Shadow's favourite board game and why?

281. What does my Shadow like best about me?

282. What do I like best about my Shadow?

283. What does my Shadow do to care for me?

284. How could my Shadow meet my needs more effectively?

285. What do I do to care for my Shadow?

286. How can I meet my Shadow's needs more effectively?

287. What's the most surprising thing I've learned about myself through Shadow Work and Play?

288. What's the most empowering thing I've learned through Shadow Work and Play?

289. In what ways do I feel creatively inspired by my Shadow?

290. What parts of myself have I been tempted to bury in my Shadow lately?

291. How would I describe my Shadow to someone else?

292. What self-reflection or spiritual practices help me connect to my Shadow?

293. Is there a certain time of day when I feel like my Shadow is more active than others?

294. How can I be physically present with my Shadow today?

295. If I could take my Shadow on a date, where would we go?

296. If my Shadow could take me on a date, where would we go?

297. How can I apply what I've learned about being compassionate with myself and my Shadow to my other relationships?

298. How has my life changed since I first started my Shadow Work journey?

299. What might I say to my Shadow if I thought I'd never see it again?

300. What do I wish I'd known about my Shadow sooner?

301. When was the last time I indulged my Shadow?

302. What did I dream of last night, and how might I read it as a message from my Shadow?

303. What does caring for myself and my Shadow look like today?

304. What progress have my Shadow and I made together recently?

305. What commitments have I made to my Shadow, and how have I been honouring them?

306. Have I been experiencing any conflict with my Shadow – or in my Shadow Work journey lately?

307. What would my Shadow like to teach me today?

308. If my Shadow were to give me a gift, what would it be?

309. If I could offer my Shadow a gift, what would I offer?

310. How do my Shadow and I protect each other?

311. What kind of life am I co-creating with my Shadow?

312. What experiences, feelings, desires or impulses are my Shadow and I ready to release?

313. What seeds for growth do I want to plant with my Shadow?

314. What new horizons is my Shadow calling me to explore?

315. How can I commune with my Shadow today?

316. What impulses do I want to risk pursuing, instead of burying them in my Shadow?

317. How can I give myself and my Shadow a break today?

318. What unexpected direction is my Shadow pulling me in?

319. How can I practise acknowledging and expressing my sadness instead of burying it in my Shadow?

320. What feels true for me and my Shadow today?

321. What has engaging with my Shadow helped me to achieve?

322. How can I renew the commitments I've made to my Shadow today?

323. What messages from my Shadow am I missing/ avoiding?

324. What happens when I feel isolated from my Shadow?

325. Have I been triggered to neglect or misuse my Shadow lately?

326. What does my regular Shadow Work practice look like right now?

327. Is there any resentment between my Shadow and me right now?

328. Have I tried to get away with burying anything in my Shadow recently?

329. What difficult feelings do I need to hold space for right now?

330. How can I turn to my Shadow for comfort right now?

331. How can I see my Shadow from a new perspective today?

332. How can my Shadow and I turn over a new leaf on our journey together?

333. What has flourished in my life as a result of engaging with my Shadow?

334. What am I most proud of about my Shadow journey so far?

335. How do I ground and support myself while working with my Shadow?

336. What does my Shadow have to teach me about courage?

337. What do my Shadow and I need to work together to bring to light?

338. What knowledge have I gained about the world through my personal Shadow Work journey?

339. What wisdom does my Shadow want to share with me today?

340. How has engaging with my Shadow helped me challenge what I was conditioned to believe about myself and the world?

341. What is holding me back from exploring my Shadow even deeper?

342. What has my Shadow been drawing my attention to recently?

343. What do I imagine is waiting beyond the parts of my Shadow I've come to know so far?

344. What skills or knowledge could I pursue to help me understand my Shadow on a deeper level?

345. What victories have I experienced with my Shadow lately?

346. What do I value most about my Shadow?

347. How do I balance my Shadow practice with my daily life?

348. Am I asking too much of my Shadow right now?

349. What old misbeliefs about my Shadow am I still working to release?

350. What did I learn early on about my Shadow, and how can I find new wisdom in that knowledge now?

351. Does being more aware of my Shadow help me avoid burnout?

352. Where do I feel stuck in my Shadow journey?

353. What is exciting me in my Shadow journey right now?

354. What are my Shadow and I struggling with together right now?

355. What has been trying to rise out of my Shadow lately?

356. Do I trust my Shadow? Does it trust me?

357. What aspects of my Shadow are still a mystery to me?

358. What makes my relationship with my Shadow a good partnership?

359. Have I been fair to my Shadow recently?

360. How can I be compassionate with my Shadow today?

361. What is it time to go searching in my Shadow for?

362. What would my Shadow and I do if we could run away together?

363. What part of my Shadow journey do I need to sit still with and reflect on?

364. What's the most recent epiphany I had about my Shadow?

365. What is next for me and my Shadow?

ABOUT THE AUTHOR

Chelsey Pippin Mizzi is a writer, tarot reader and certified Shadow Work practitioner (accredited through the Complementary Medical Association) based in the south of France. Her writing has been featured in BuzzFeed, *METRO*, *New York Magazine*, *The Bookseller* and other titles. She publishes *The Shuffle*, an independent magazine at the intersection of creativity and spirituality at theshuffle.substack. com.

The Shadow Path is her third book, following on from *The Tarot Spreads Yearbook* and *Tarot for Creativity*.

Follow Chelsey on Instagram at @pipcardstarot.

ACKNOWLEDGEMENTS

This book, like all of my other writing, would be impossible without my friends and colleagues at the London Writers' Salon. Your reliable camaraderie, support and knowledge-sharing have made all the difference in keeping me afloat, in my creative practice and in my life.

Many thanks are due to the team that helped me bring this book together: notably, my agent Jane Graham Maw and my editors Lucy Carroll and Cara Waudby-Tolley. I'm eternally grateful for all of your faith, cheerleading and guidance throughout this process.

I am in so much creative debt to my coaching, tarot and mentoring clients. Thank you for trusting me as a companion on your journeys. I love spending time in your worlds, and helping you unlock creativity, joy and curiosity. It feeds me and inspires me all the time.

Thank you to everyone who reads and recommends my work in any format. I am especially grateful to the full-access and founding subscribers to my newsletter, *The Shuffle*. Your support fuels the work I do there, but it also makes my broader efforts – like writing books – possible. I'm blessed to be in community with you.

Thank you to Lillie Jamieson and the whole team at Send it to Alex, for being the most supportive and understanding 'day job' a neurodivergent writer could dream of.

I am lucky to have friends around the world who understand that I disappear for months on end while on deadline, and cheerfully accept my need to moan about my passions. In particular, thank you to Kat Dunn and Sara Gray, for being there since before the beginning, and for always holding space for me to process the ups and downs of life and publishing. Thanks to Rebecca and Sarah for being grounding presences in Avignon and for many co-working sessions. To Nix Palomba, for a much-needed tarot reading as I bumped up against the end of a year and the final stages of drafting.

To my family – the Pippins, Crabtrees, Mizzis and all the threads that stem from there: I am deeply touched by your enthusiasm for my writing and your support as I muddle through it. You have all my love and all my thanks.

Finally, thank you always to Zacharie Mizzi, Fletcher and Figg, anchors I wouldn't trade for anything.